100 Vocabulary Quizzes

with
Weekly Planner

MentaFlex Learning

[1] George A. Miller (1995). WordNet: A Lexical Database for English. Communications of the ACM Vol. 38, No. 11: 39-41.

[2] Christiane Fellbaum (1998, ed.) WordNet: An Electronic Lexical Database. Cambridge, MA: MIT Press.

[3] https://wordnet.princeton.edu/wordnet/license/

This workbook contains 1,500 English words that are commonly used in everyday communication, mass media, literature, and standardized tests. Each page represents a vocabulary quiz with fifteen words that need to be matched with their definitions. The words are provided on the top of the page numbered 1-15. The reader needs to write the numbers in the answer boxes corresponding to their definitions. The alternate pages of the workbook represent a weekly planner with a note area.

CONTENTS

1
Quizzes

Quiz 1

1 issuing	6 purport	11 wearing
2 accomplice	7 repository	12 cheater
3 cosmology	8 nervousness	13 destitute
4 beginner	9 ventilation	14 upshot
5 untrained	10 intrinsically	15 enliven

- [ ] A person who joins with another in carrying out some plan
- [ ] The metaphysical study of the origin and nature of the universe
- [ ] With respect to its inherent nature
- [ ] Producing exhaustion
- [ ] Heighten or intensify
- [ ] Have the often specious appearance of being, intending, or claiming
- [ ] The act of supplying fresh air and getting rid of foul air
- [ ] The act of providing an item for general use or for official purposes
- [ ] The anxious feeling you have when you have the jitters
- [ ] Someone new to a field or activity
- [ ] Not disciplined, conditioned or made adept by training
- [ ] A phenomenon that follows and is caused by some previous phenomenon
- [ ] Poor enough to need help from others
- [ ] Someone who leads you to believe something that is not true
- [ ] A facility where things can be deposited for storage or safekeeping

Week #_______ From ____/____/_____ to ____/____/_____

Date	Weekday	Morning	Afternoon	Evening
	Monday			
	Tuesday			
	Wednesday			
	Thursday			
	Friday			
	Saturday			
	Sunday			

Notes

1	momentary	6	antagonism	11	ascertain
2	vagueness	7	helix	12	seismic
3	uneventful	8	slant	13	mileage
4	decreased	9	underpin	14	participating
5	meteorite	10	chimpanzee	15	robotics

☐ A state of deep-seated ill-will

☐ Distance measured in miles

☐ A curve that lies on the surface of a cylinder or cone and cuts the element at a constant angle

☐ The area of artificial intelligence concerned with the practical use of robots

☐ Taking part in an activity

☐ Subject to or caused by an earthquake or earth vibration

☐ Stony or metallic object that is the remains of a meteoroid that has reached the Earth's surface

☐ Marked by no noteworthy or significant events

☐ Made less in size, amount or degree

☐ Unclearness by virtue of being poorly expressed or not coherent in meaning

☐ Establish after a calculation, investigation, experiment, survey, or study

☐ Intelligent somewhat arboreal ape of equatorial African forests

☐ Lasting for a markedly brief time

☐ Support from beneath

☐ A biased way of looking at or presenting something

Week #_______ From _____/_____/_____ to _____/_____/_____

Date	Weekday	Morning	Afternoon	Evening
	Monday			
	Tuesday			
	Wednesday			
	Thursday			
	Friday			
	Saturday			
	Sunday			

Notes

1 exterior	6 blower	11 incline
2 infest	7 tributary	12 dreaded
3 microcosm	8 materialism	13 underserved
4 bacillus	9 anachronism	14 vaporize
5 outermost	10 symbiosis	15 nimble

☐ Have a tendency or disposition to do or be something; be inclined

☐ A device that produces a current of air

☐ Invade in great numbers

☐ Not having sufficient service

☐ The relation between two different species of organisms that are interdependent; each gains benefits from the other

☐ The region that is outside of something

☐ A miniature model of something

☐ Situated at the farthest possible point from a center

☐ Aerobic rod-shaped spore-producing bacterium; often occurring in chainlike formations; found primarily in soil

☐ Causing fear, dread or terror

☐ Flowing into a larger stream

☐ Something located at a time when it could not have existed or occurred

☐ A desire for wealth and material possessions with little interest in ethical or spiritual matters

☐ Moving quickly and lightly

☐ Kill with or as if with a burst of gunfire or electric current or as if by shooting

Week #_____ From ____/____/____ to ____/____/____

Date	Weekday	Morning	Afternoon	Evening
	Monday			
	Tuesday			
	Wednesday			
	Thursday			
	Friday			
	Saturday			
	Sunday			

Notes

1 irresistible	6 partake	11 toxicity
2 murky	7 evergreen	12 inscribed
3 mitigate	8 grapevine	13 decontamination
4 labyrinthine	9 rearrangement	14 handbook
5 incursion	10 spartan	15 undetected

☐ Bearing foliage throughout the year

☐ The removal of contaminants

☐ Clouded as with sediment

☐ Resolute in the face of pain, danger or adversity

☐ Impossible to resist; overpowering

☐ The degree to which something is poisonous

☐ Written on or in a surface

☐ Gossip spread by spoken communication

☐ Have some of the qualities or attributes of something

☐ Relating to, affecting or originating in the inner ear

☐ A concise reference book providing specific information about a subject or location

☐ Changing an arrangement

☐ Lessen or to try to lessen the seriousness or extent of

☐ Not perceived or discerned

☐ The act of entering some territory or domain

Week #_______ From ____/____/____ to ____/____/____

Date	Weekday	Morning	Afternoon	Evening
	Monday			
	Tuesday			
	Wednesday			
	Thursday			
	Friday			
	Saturday			
	Sunday			

Notes

➤
➤
➤
➤
➤
➤
➤
➤
➤
➤
➤
➤
➤
➤
➤
➤
➤
➤

1 drumming	6 refinery	11 overstate
2 quotation	7 irregularity	12 plateau
3 cannibal	8 tinker	13 manic
4 loot	9 disenchantment	14 ecologist
5 appease	10 hefty	15 quarantine

☐ Goods or money obtained illegally

☐ The act of playing drums

☐ Do random, unplanned work, activities or spend time idly

☐ A biologist who studies the relation between organisms and their environment

☐ A person who eats human flesh

☐ Enforced isolation of patients suffering from a contagious disease in order to prevent the spread of disease

☐ To enlarge beyond bounds or the truth

☐ Possessing physical strength and weight; rugged and powerful

☐ A short note recognizing a source of information or of a quoted passage

☐ Cause to be more favorably inclined; gain the good will of

☐ Behavior that breaches the rule, etiquette, custom or morality

☐ An industrial plant for purifying a crude substance

☐ Affected with or marked by frenzy or mania uncontrolled by reason

☐ Disappointment on finding out that something is not as good as hoped, or that previous beliefs were false

☐ A relatively flat highland

Week #______ From ____/____/____ to ____/____/____

Date	Weekday	Morning	Afternoon	Evening
	Monday			
	Tuesday			
	Wednesday			
	Thursday			
	Friday			
	Saturday			
	Sunday			

Notes

1 anecdote	6 embodiment	11 coherence
2 commonsense	7 inverted	12 steward
3 metabolism	8 emblematic	13 blemish
4 coma	9 dissuade	14 seductive
5 horrific	10 conceit	15 inclination

☐ A short, interesting or amusing account of a real incident

☐ Being in such a position that top and bottom are reversed

☐ The marked and rapid transformation of a larva into an adult that occurs in some animals

☐ Exhibiting native good judgment

☐ Turn away from by persuasion

☐ Logical, orderly, and consistent relation of parts

☐ A state of deep and often prolonged unconsciousness; usually the result of disease or injury

☐ Tending to entice into a desired action or state

☐ A new personification of a familiar idea

☐ An attitude of mind especially one that favors one alternative over others

☐ Feelings of excessive pride

☐ Serving as a visible symbol for something abstract

☐ Someone who manages property or other affairs for someone else

☐ Grossly offensive to decency or morality; causing horror

☐ A mark or flaw that spoils the appearance of something

Week #_______ From ____/____/____ to ____/____/____

Date	Weekday	Morning	Afternoon	Evening
	Monday			
	Tuesday			
	Wednesday			
	Thursday			
	Friday			
	Saturday			
	Sunday			

Notes

1	foreground	6	subvert	11	workload
2	streamlined	7	exploitative	12	disengage
3	sampler	8	rime	13	onerous
4	rationalize	9	everlasting	14	coffer
5	repeat	10	ingenious	15	noninvasive

☐ Made efficient by stripping off nonessentials

☐ Ice crystals forming a white deposit

☐ The part of a scene that is near the viewer

☐ Continuing forever or indefinitely

☐ An observation station that is set up to make sample observations of something

☐ Cause the downfall of; of rulers

☐ Imposing or constituting a physical, mental, or figurative load which can be borne only with effort

☐ Relating to a technique that does not involve puncturing the skin or entering a body cavity

☐ Showing inventiveness and skill

☐ To say, state, or perform again

☐ Release from something that holds fast, connects, or entangles

☐ An ornamental sunken panel in a ceiling or dome

☐ Tending to exploit or make use of

☐ Defend, explain, clear away, or make excuses for by reasoning

☐ Work that a person is expected to do in a specified time

Week #_______ From _____/_____/_____ to _____/_____/_____

Date	Weekday	Morning	Afternoon	Evening
	Monday			
	Tuesday			
	Wednesday			
	Thursday			
	Friday			
	Saturday			
	Sunday			

Notes

1 layperson	6 extrapolation	11 depleted
2 subversion	7 prehistory	12 retraction
3 tessellation	8 aqueduct	13 interdiction
4 purveyor	9 disorderly	14 rung
5 traumatize	10 dummy	15 perverse

☐ No longer sufficient

☐ A crosspiece between the legs of a chair

☐ A conduit that resembles a bridge but carries water over a valley

☐ Destroying someone's honesty or loyalty; undermining moral integrity

☐ A disavowal or taking back of a previous assertion

☐ Someone who is not a clergyman or a professional person

☐ The careful juxtaposition of shapes in a pattern

☐ Calculation of the value of a function outside the range of known values

☐ Authoritative prohibition

☐ Undisciplined and unruly

☐ The time during the development of human culture before the appearance of the written word

☐ A person who does not talk

☐ Marked by a disposition to oppose and contradict

☐ Inflict a trauma upon

☐ Someone who supplies provisions

Week #_______ From ____/____/____   to ____/____/____

Date	Weekday	Morning	Afternoon	Evening
	Monday			
	Tuesday			
	Wednesday			
	Thursday			
	Friday			
	Saturday			
	Sunday			

Notes

1 wearer	6 spasm	11 secularism
2 nationalization	7 reddish	12 lightness
3 omission	8 iconography	13 perennial
4 dermatologist	9 contentious	14 refuse
5 malady	10 puncture	15 contentment

☐ A doctor who specializes in the physiology and pathology of the skin

☐ Happiness with one's situation in life

☐ A mistake resulting from neglect

☐ Lasting three seasons or more

☐ A feeling of joy and pride

☐ A doctrine that rejects religion and religious considerations

☐ Of a color at the end of the color spectrum; resembling the color of blood, cherries, tomatoes or rubies

☐ Inclined or showing an inclination to dispute or disagree, even to engage in law suits

☐ The action of forming or becoming a nation

☐ A person who wears or carries or displays something as a body covering or accessory

☐ Show unwillingness towards

☐ Pierce with a pointed object; make a hole into

☐ A painful and involuntary muscular contraction

☐ The images and symbolic representations that are traditionally associated with a person or a subject

☐ Any unwholesome or desperate condition

Week #______ From _____/_____/_____ to _____/_____/_____

Date	Weekday	Morning	Afternoon	Evening
	Monday			
	Tuesday			
	Wednesday			
	Thursday			
	Friday			
	Saturday			
	Sunday			

Notes

1	lexicon	6	shun	11	runaway
2	powered	7	resilient	12	transformative
3	salamander	8	reconstitute	13	psychosis
4	angina	9	incremental	14	fluorescence
5	thoracic	10	crucify	15	warship

- [ ] Light emitted during absorption of radiation of some other wavelength
- [ ] Having or using or propelled by means of power or power of a specified kind
- [ ] Of or relating to the chest or thorax
- [ ] Any severe mental disorder in which contact with reality is lost or highly distorted
- [ ] Any of various typically terrestrial amphibians that resemble lizards and that return to water only to breed
- [ ] A reference work containing a list of words in alphabetical order, giving their meaning and other information
- [ ] Recovering readily from adversity, depression, or the like
- [ ] Kill by nailing onto a cross
- [ ] Any disease of the throat or fauces marked by spasmodic attacks of intense suffocative pain
- [ ] Completely out of control
- [ ] Avoid and stay away from deliberately; stay clear of
- [ ] Construct or form a new or provide with a new structure
- [ ] A government ship that is available for waging war
- [ ] Having power, or a tendency, to transform
- [ ] Increasing gradually by regular degrees or additions

Week #_____ From ____/____/____ to ____/____/____

Date	Weekday	Morning	Afternoon	Evening
	Monday			
	Tuesday			
	Wednesday			
	Thursday			
	Friday			
	Saturday			
	Sunday			

Notes

Quiz 11

1 amorous	6 retarded	11 incurable
2 wellness	7 spoken	12 algae
3 complicity	8 plainly	13 feeding
4 consolidation	9 conscript	14 bonanza
5 strangeness	10 normality	15 parenthood

☐ Inclined toward or displaying love

☐ Relatively slow in mental, emotional or physical development

☐ Unmistakably; visibly clear; in an evident manner

☐ Unusualness as a consequence of not being well known

☐ Guilt as an accomplice in a crime or offence

☐ Enroll into service compulsorily

☐ The state of being free of physical or psychological disease, illness, or malfunction

☐ Uttered through the medium of speech or characterized by speech; sometimes used in combination

☐ The state of being a parent

☐ Primitive chlorophyll-containing mainly aquatic eukaryotic organisms lacking true stems and roots and leaves

☐ Being within certain limits that define the range of normal functioning

☐ Incapable of being cured

☐ The act of consuming food

☐ A sudden happening that brings good fortune

☐ Combining into a solid mass

Week #_____ From ____/____/____ to ____/____/____

Date	Weekday	Morning	Afternoon	Evening
	Monday			
	Tuesday			
	Wednesday			
	Thursday			
	Friday			
	Saturday			
	Sunday			

Notes

Quiz **12**

1 contrived	6 headaddress	11 transfusion
2 clot	7 rustic	12 ensue
3 cursory	8 disenchanted	13 chisel
4 adornment	9 interweave	14 stiffness
5 paramilitary	10 mute	15 revealing

☐ A decoration of color or interest that is added to relieve plainness

☐ Showing effects of planning or manipulation

☐ Clothing for the head

☐ Happen afterwards as a consequence

☐ A lump of material formed from the content of a liquid

☐ Characteristic of rural life

☐ Of or relating to a group of civilians organized to function like or to assist a military unit

☐ Expressed without speech

☐ The physical property of being inflexible and hard to bend

☐ Hasty and without attention to detail; not thorough

☐ Freed from enchantment

☐ Disclosing unintentionally

☐ Interlace by or as if by weaving

☐ An edge tool with a flat steel blade with a cutting edge

☐ The introduction of blood or blood plasma into a vein or artery

Week #_______ From _____/_____/_____ to _____/_____/_____

Date	Weekday	Morning	Afternoon	Evening
	Monday			
	Tuesday			
	Wednesday			
	Thursday			
	Friday			
	Saturday			
	Sunday			

Notes

1 satirical	6 headway	11 unquestioned
2 neuroscience	7 appalling	12 vowel
3 collecting	8 bystander	13 dismemberment
4 hibernation	9 backbone	14 pessimist
5 fence	10 evaporation	15 quare

- [ ] Vertical space available to allow easy passage under something
- [ ] A central cohesive source of support and stability
- [ ] The torpid or resting state in which some animals pass the winter
- [ ] A barrier that serves to enclose an area
- [ ] A speech sound made with the vocal tract open
- [ ] Exposing human folly to ridicule
- [ ] Generally agreed upon; not subject to dispute
- [ ] The removal of limbs; being cut to pieces
- [ ] A nonparticipant spectator
- [ ] The defendant unlawfully enters the land of the plaintiff
- [ ] Causing consternation
- [ ] The act of gathering something together
- [ ] The process of becoming a vapor
- [ ] The scientific study of the nervous system
- [ ] A person who expects the worst

Week #_____ From ____/____/____ to ____/____/____

Date	Weekday	Morning	Afternoon	Evening
	Monday			
	Tuesday			
	Wednesday			
	Thursday			
	Friday			
	Saturday			
	Sunday			

Notes

➤
➤
➤
➤
➤
➤
➤
➤
➤
➤
➤
➤
➤
➤
➤
➤
➤
➤
➤

1 pelican	6 interfaith	11 vent
2 lifeline	7 reservist	12 minute
3 auxiliary	8 frieze	13 legible
4 unsupported	9 lycopene	14 unending
5 subjugation	10 wishful	15 havoc

☐ Capable of being read or deciphered

☐ Violent and needless disturbance

☐ Forced submission to control by others

☐ A hole for the escape of gas or air

☐ An architectural ornament consisting of a horizontal sculptured band between the architrave and the cornice

☐ A member of a military reserve

☐ Someone who acts as assistant

☐ Carotenoid that makes tomatoes red; may lower the risk of prostate cancer

☐ A crease on the palm; its length is said by palmists to indicate how long you will live

☐ A unit of time equal to 60 seconds or 1/60th of an hour

☐ Not sustained or maintained by nonmaterial aid

☐ Involving persons of different religious faiths

☐ Continuing forever or indefinitely

☐ Large long-winged warm-water seabird having a large bill with a distensible pouch for fish

☐ Having or expressing desire for something

Week #_______ From _____/_____/_____ to _____/_____/_____

Date	Weekday	Morning	Afternoon	Evening
	Monday			
	Tuesday			
	Wednesday			
	Thursday			
	Friday			
	Saturday			
	Sunday			

Notes

1 sighting	6 android	11 illegitimate
2 modernize	7 plywood	12 superconductor
3 misnomer	8 loaded	13 sterilization
4 panorama	9 normalization	14 existential
5 fascia	10 transformer	15 emanate

☐ An incorrect or unsuitable name

☐ A material that has no electric resistance

☐ A laminate made of thin layers of wood

☐ Contrary to or forbidden by law

☐ An electrical device by which alternating current of one voltage is changed to another voltage

☐ The act of making an organism barren or infertile

☐ The act of observing

☐ Make repairs, renovations, revisions or adjustments to

☐ The imposition of standards or regulations

☐ A sheet or band of fibrous connective tissue separating or binding together muscles and organs etc

☐ Derived from experience or the experience of existence

☐ A distant view of a wide area, especially one that is pleasant to look at

☐ Filled with a great quantity

☐ Proceed or issue forth, as from a source

☐ An automaton that resembles a human being

Week #_______ From ____/____/____   to ____/____/____

Date	Weekday	Morning	Afternoon	Evening
	Monday			
	Tuesday			
	Wednesday			
	Thursday			
	Friday			
	Saturday			
	Sunday			

Notes

1	roadway	6	paralysis	11	subversive
2	scapegoat	7	degraded	12	scavenger
3	truce	8	disorganization	13	rhythmic
4	wiring	9	acronym	14	playful
5	outcry	10	microbiology	15	opus

☐ Loss of the ability to move a body part

☐ A circuit of wires for the distribution of electricity

☐ Full of fun and high spirits

☐ A musical work that has been created

☐ A condition in which an orderly system has been disrupted

☐ Unrestrained by convention or morality

☐ In opposition to a civil authority or government

☐ The branch of biology that studies microorganisms and their effects on humans

☐ Recurring with measured regularity

☐ Someone who is punished for the errors of others

☐ A chemical agent that is added to a chemical mixture to counteract the effects of impurities

☐ A word formed from the initial letters of the several words in the name

☐ A loud utterance; often in protest or opposition

☐ A state of peace agreed to between opponents so they can discuss peace terms

☐ A road over which vehicles travel

Week #_____ From ____/____/____ to ____/____/____

Date	Weekday	Morning	Afternoon	Evening
	Monday			
	Tuesday			
	Wednesday			
	Thursday			
	Friday			
	Saturday			
	Sunday			

Notes

➢
➢
➢
➢
➢
➢
➢
➢
➢
➢
➢
➢
➢
➢
➢
➢
➢
➢

1	symbiotic	6	splendor	11	twisting
2	matte	7	fresco	12	criminology
3	purposely	8	scant	13	entwine
4	polemical	9	extramarital	14	drudgery
5	palate	10	grassland	15	preserve

☐ A mural done with watercolors on wet plaster

☐ With intention; in an intentional manner

☐ A quality that outshines the usual

☐ The scientific study of crime and criminal behavior and law enforcement

☐ Hard monotonous routine work

☐ Land where grass or grasslike vegetation grows and is the dominant form of plant life

☐ Tie or link together

☐ Not reflecting light; not glossy

☐ Keep or maintain in unaltered condition; cause to remain or last

☐ The act of distorting something so it seems to mean something it was not intended to mean

☐ Less than the correct, legal or full amount, often deliberately

☐ The upper surface of the mouth that separates the oral and nasal cavities

☐ Living together, usually to their mutual advantage

☐ Of or involving dispute or controversy

☐ Characterized by adultery

Week #_____ From ____/____/____ to ____/____/____

Date	Weekday	Morning	Afternoon	Evening
	Monday			
	Tuesday			
	Wednesday			
	Thursday			
	Friday			
	Saturday			
	Sunday			

Notes

1 pancreas	6 abscess	11 utopia
2 dweller	7 melatonin	12 masculinity
3 precondition	8 misguided	13 protector
4 fiasco	9 atrophy	14 politicize
5 subside	10 conical	15 arithmetic

☐ A decrease in size of an organ caused by disease or disuse

☐ Hormone secreted by the pineal gland

☐ The properties characteristic of the male sex

☐ A disastrous or embarrassing failure

☐ Wear off or die down

☐ A person who inhabits a particular place

☐ The branch of pure mathematics dealing with the theory of numerical calculations

☐ Give a political character to

☐ Poorly conceived or thought out

☐ A large elongated exocrine gland located behind the stomach; secretes pancreatic juice and insulin

☐ Relating to or resembling a cone

☐ Symptom consisting of a localized collection of pus surrounded by inflamed tissue

☐ A person who cares for persons or property

☐ Put into the required condition beforehand

☐ Ideally perfect state; especially in its social and political and moral aspects

Week #_______ From _____/_____/_____ to _____/_____/_____

Date	Weekday	Morning	Afternoon	Evening
	Monday			
	Tuesday			
	Wednesday			
	Thursday			
	Friday			
	Saturday			
	Sunday			

Notes

1	purification	6	adage	11	steamer
2	balk	7	nave	12	saline
3	paranormal	8	coordinating	13	viability
4	undoing	9	carnival	14	number
5	partisanship	10	circumference	15	brunt

☐ Serving to connect two grammatical constituents of identical construction

☐ The act of cleaning by getting rid of impurities

☐ An isotonic solution of sodium chloride and distilled water

☐ The size of something as given by the distance around it

☐ The full adverse effects of; the chief consequences or negative results of a thing or event

☐ An inclination to favor one group, view or opinion over alternatives

☐ The property possessed by a sum or total or indefinite quantity of units or individuals

☐ An act that makes a previous act of no effect

☐ Capable of normal growth and development

☐ Seemingly outside normal sensory channels

☐ A clam that is usually steamed in the shell

☐ A condensed saying embodying some important fact of experience that is taken as true by many people

☐ Pause or hold back in uncertainty or unwillingness

☐ The central area of a church

☐ A festival marked by merrymaking and processions

Week #______ From ____/____/____ to ____/____/____

Date	Weekday	Morning	Afternoon	Evening
	Monday			
	Tuesday			
	Wednesday			
	Thursday			
	Friday			
	Saturday			
	Sunday			

Notes

1	monoxide	6	rotator	11	following
2	humility	7	dearth	12	hindrance
3	emptiness	8	codex	13	insensitive
4	viral	9	discernible	14	hugely
5	disordered	10	disbursement	15	watchful

☐ Thrown into a state of disarray or confusion

☐ Amounts paid for goods and services that may be currently tax deductible

☐ Not responsive to physical stimuli

☐ An official list of chemicals or medicines

☐ Used as an intensifier

☐ Engaged in or accustomed to close observation

☐ An oxide containing just one atom of oxygen in the molecule

☐ The state of containing nothing

☐ A disposition to be humble; a lack of false pride

☐ Relating to or caused by a virus

☐ Something that interferes with action or progress

☐ An acute insufficiency

☐ A revolving reverberatory furnace

☐ About to be mentioned or specified

☐ Perceptible by the senses or intellect

Week #_____ From ____/____/____ to ____/____/____

Date	Weekday	Morning	Afternoon	Evening
	Monday			
	Tuesday			
	Wednesday			
	Thursday			
	Friday			
	Saturday			
	Sunday			

Notes

1 understate	6 earmark	11 dismissal
2 scorn	7 pale	12 smuggling
3 encode	8 thermometer	13 pertinent
4 versatile	9 stretching	14 demo
5 surmise	10 blackboard	15 inflate

☐ A visual presentation showing how something works

☐ Having precise or logical relevance to the matter at hand

☐ A judgment disposing of the matter without a trial

☐ Act of expanding by lengthening or widening

☐ Sheet of slate; for writing with chalk

☐ Convert information into code

☐ Exaggerate or make bigger

☐ Give or assign a resource to a particular person or cause

☐ Very light colored; highly diluted with white

☐ Measuring instrument for measuring temperature

☐ Secretly importing prohibited goods or goods on which duty is due

☐ Infer from incomplete evidence

☐ Lack of respect accompanied by a feeling of intense dislike

☐ Having great diversity or variety

☐ Represent as less significant or important

Week #_______ From ____/____/____ to ____/____/____

Date	Weekday	Morning	Afternoon	Evening
	Monday			
	Tuesday			
	Wednesday			
	Thursday			
	Friday			
	Saturday			
	Sunday			

Notes

1 underside	6 brainchild	11 jargon
2 exuberant	7 looter	12 fecundity
3 belie	8 citizenry	13 offence
4 solid	9 eugenics	14 unprotected
5 austerity	10 lyrical	15 unworkable

☐ The study of methods of improving genetic qualities by selective breeding

☐ Not capable of being carried out or put into practice

☐ Someone who takes spoils or plunder

☐ The body of citizens of a state or country

☐ A characteristic language of a particular group

☐ Be in contradiction with

☐ Lacking protection or defense

☐ A product of your creative thinking and work

☐ The intellectual productivity of a creative imagination

☐ A lack of politeness; a failure to show regard for others; wounding the feelings or others

☐ Characterized by good substantial quality

☐ The trait of great self-denial

☐ Joyously unrestrained

☐ The lower side of anything

☐ Suitable for or suggestive of singing

Week #_____ From ____/____/____ to ____/____/____

Date	Weekday	Morning	Afternoon	Evening
	Monday			
	Tuesday			
	Wednesday			
	Thursday			
	Friday			
	Saturday			
	Sunday			

Notes

1 insurrection	6 unwritten	11 underdeveloped
2 puny	7 striker	12 programmer
3 hamper	8 trance	13 deplore
4 playback	9 moniker	14 axle
5 abreast	10 modesty	15 gratification

- [ ] Being up to particular standard or level especially in being up to date in knowledge
- [ ] Based on custom rather than documentation
- [ ] Relating to societies in which capital needed to industrialize is in short supply
- [ ] Inferior in strength or significance
- [ ] A familiar name for a person
- [ ] A forward on a soccer team
- [ ] Organized opposition to authority; a conflict in which one faction tries to wrest control from another
- [ ] The act of reproducing recorded sound
- [ ] A person who designs and writes and tests computer programs
- [ ] A psychological state induced by a magical incantation
- [ ] Express strong disapproval of
- [ ] Freedom from vanity or conceit
- [ ] A shaft on which a wheel rotates
- [ ] State of being gratified or satisfied
- [ ] Prevent the progress or free movement of

Week #_____ From ____/____/____ to ____/____/____

Date	Weekday	Morning	Afternoon	Evening
	Monday			
	Tuesday			
	Wednesday			
	Thursday			
	Friday			
	Saturday			
	Sunday			

Notes

1	fortuitous	6	radiologist	11	arbiter
2	germ	7	punitive	12	reliant
3	extortion	8	gymnastics	13	simplification
4	quarrel	9	reconstructive	14	tolerant
5	suitor	10	hypocritical	15	insulate

- [ ] Showing respect for the rights, opinions or practices of others
- [ ] A man who courts a woman
- [ ] Professing feelings or virtues one does not have
- [ ] An exorbitant charge
- [ ] A medical specialist who uses radioactive substances and X-rays in the treatment of disease
- [ ] A sport that involves exercises intended to display strength and balance and agility
- [ ] Helping to restore to good condition
- [ ] An explanation that omits superfluous details and reduces complexity
- [ ] Protect from heat, cold, or noise by surrounding with insulating material
- [ ] Inflicting punishment
- [ ] Having no cause or apparent cause
- [ ] Anything that provides inspiration for later work
- [ ] Have a disagreement over something
- [ ] Someone with the power to settle matters at will
- [ ] Relying on another for support

Week #_______ From ____/____/____ to ____/____/____

Date	Weekday	Morning	Afternoon	Evening
	Monday			
	Tuesday			
	Wednesday			
	Thursday			
	Friday			
	Saturday			
	Sunday			

Notes

1 ingest	6 commoner	11 flux
2 rupture	7 downgrade	12 disjunction
3 linguistics	8 refutation	13 bravo
4 motivated	9 caddy	14 evangelicalism
5 extracurricular	10 infallible	15 civility

☐ State of being disconnected

☐ A can for storing tea

☐ The speech act of answering an attack on your assertions

☐ Stresses the importance of personal conversion and faith as the means of salvation

☐ Separate or cause to separate abruptly

☐ A murderer who kills by a surprise attack and often is hired to do the deed

☐ A person who holds no title

☐ To take into the body, as for digestion

☐ Outside the regular academic curriculum

☐ Provided with a motive or given incentive for action

☐ The scientific study of language

☐ Incapable of failure or error

☐ Rate lower; lower in value or esteem

☐ Formal or perfunctory politeness

☐ The rate of flow of energy or particles across a given surface

Week #______   From ____/____/____   to ____/____/____

Date	Weekday	Morning	Afternoon	Evening
	Monday			
	Tuesday			
	Wednesday			
	Thursday			
	Friday			
	Saturday			
	Sunday			

Notes

➤
➤
➤
➤
➤
➤
➤
➤
➤
➤
➤
➤
➤
➤
➤
➤
➤
➤
➤

1 increment	6 revere	11 gerontology
2 optimize	7 loudspeaker	12 agribusiness
3 folio	8 homogeneous	13 absorption
4 nomadic	9 capitulation	14 nothingness
5 beehive	10 interconnected	15 ethnocentrism

☐ A large-scale farming enterprise

☐ The system of numbering pages

☐ Make optimal; get the most out of; use best

☐ Belief in the superiority of one's own ethnic group

☐ A document containing the terms of surrender

☐ Any workplace where people are very busy

☐ Electro-acoustic transducer that converts electrical signals into sounds loud enough to be heard at a distance

☐ The state of nonexistence

☐ The branch of medical science that deals with diseases and problems specific to old people

☐ A process in which one substance permeates another; a fluid permeates or is dissolved by a liquid or solid

☐ Reciprocally connected

☐ All of the same or similar kind or nature

☐ Love unquestioningly and uncritically or to excess; venerate as an idol

☐ Having no fixed home; changing location regularly as required for work or food

☐ A process of becoming larger or longer or more numerous or more important

Week #_______ From _____/_____/_____ to _____/_____/_____

Date	Weekday	Morning	Afternoon	Evening
	Monday			
	Tuesday			
	Wednesday			
	Thursday			
	Friday			
	Saturday			
	Sunday			

Notes

1	overdo	6	understatement	11	vengeful
2	informative	7	remission	12	swelling
3	metaphoric	8	decompose	13	traction
4	cunning	9	author	14	orangutan
5	tack	10	rejoice	15	perpetuity

☐ Attractive especially by means of smallness, prettiness or quaintness

☐ The friction between a body and the surface on which it moves

☐ Large long-armed ape of Borneo and Sumatra having arboreal habits

☐ Feel happiness or joy

☐ Tending to increase knowledge or dissipate ignorance

☐ A statement that is restrained in ironic contrast to what might have been said

☐ Disposed to seek revenge or intended for revenge

☐ Into constituent elements or parts

☐ Expressing one thing in terms normally denoting another

☐ Do something to an excessive degree

☐ The property of being perpetual

☐ An abatement in intensity or degree

☐ An abnormal protuberance or localized enlargement

☐ A short nail with a sharp point and a large head

☐ Someone who writes professionally

Week #_____ From ____/____/____ to ____/____/____

Date	Weekday	Morning	Afternoon	Evening
	Monday			
	Tuesday			
	Wednesday			
	Thursday			
	Friday			
	Saturday			
	Sunday			

Notes

1 dermatology	6 uplifting	11 transgenic
2 skeptic	7 acupuncture	12 monotonous
3 seriousness	8 pandemic	13 purposeful
4 gentleness	9 proverb	14 underline
5 induction	10 sailing	15 absurdity

- [ ] A simple saying, popularly known and repeated, that expresses a truth based on common sense or experience
- [ ] A formal entry into an organization, position or office
- [ ] Epidemic over a wide geographical area
- [ ] Someone who habitually doubts accepted beliefs
- [ ] Something that is absurd or ridiculous; a logical contradiction
- [ ] Treatment of pain or disease by inserting the tips of needles at specific points on the skin
- [ ] The work of a sailor
- [ ] Serving as or indicating the existence of a purpose or goal
- [ ] The property possessed by a slope that is very gradual
- [ ] Tediously repetitious or lacking in variety
- [ ] Containing artificially inserted genetic material from another species
- [ ] Causing cheerfulness, happiness, hope, or moral elevation
- [ ] The branch of medicine dealing with the skin and its diseases
- [ ] Give extra weight to
- [ ] An earnest and sincere feeling

Week #_______ From ____/____/____   to ____/____/____

Date	Weekday	Morning	Afternoon	Evening
	Monday			
	Tuesday			
	Wednesday			
	Thursday			
	Friday			
	Saturday			
	Sunday			

Notes

1 labyrinth	6 fervor	11 imperative
2 lactose	7 antidote	12 outdated
3 epidermis	8 estranged	13 psychotherapist
4 martyr	9 indulgence	14 morphine
5 optimist	10 adaptability	15 admirer

- [ ] Requiring attention or action
- [ ] Complex system of paths or tunnels in which it is easy to get lost
- [ ] A sugar comprising one glucose molecule linked to a galactose molecule; occurs only in milk
- [ ] An inability to resist the gratification of whims and desires
- [ ] A remedy that stops or controls the effects of a poison
- [ ] A person who backs a politician or a team etc
- [ ] Feelings of great warmth and intensity
- [ ] A person disposed to take a favorable view of things
- [ ] A therapist who deals with mental and emotional disorders
- [ ] One who suffers for the sake of principle
- [ ] The ability to change to fit changed circumstances
- [ ] The outer layer of the skin covering the exterior body surface of vertebrates
- [ ] Caused to be unloved
- [ ] No longer valid or fashionable
- [ ] An alkaloid narcotic drug extracted from opium; a powerful, habit-forming narcotic used to relieve pain

Week #______ From ____/____/____ to ____/____/____

Date	Weekday	Morning	Afternoon	Evening
	Monday			
	Tuesday			
	Wednesday			
	Thursday			
	Friday			
	Saturday			
	Sunday			

Notes

1	subordinate	6	synthesize	11	ledger
2	supervising	7	ordered	12	detractor
3	winged	8	immersion	13	bravery
4	detritus	9	blunder	14	dynasty
5	indignation	10	secession	15	antiquity

☐ Having a systematic arrangement; especially having elements succeeding in order according to rule

☐ Combine so as to form a more complex, product

☐ Management by overseeing the performance or operation of a person or group

☐ The remains of something that has been destroyed or broken up

☐ A sequence of powerful leaders in the same family

☐ Anger aroused by some perceived offence or injustice

☐ An Austrian school of art and architecture parallel to the French art nouveau in the 1890s

☐ Sinking until covered completely with water

☐ An embarrassing mistake

☐ A record in which commercial accounts are recorded

☐ Having wings or as if having wings of a specified kind

☐ A quality of spirit that enables you to face danger or pain without showing fear

☐ The historic period preceding the Middle Ages in Europe

☐ One who disparages or belittles the worth of something

☐ An assistant subject to the authority or control of another

Week #______ From ____/____/____ to ____/____/____

Date	Weekday	Morning	Afternoon	Evening
	Monday			
	Tuesday			
	Wednesday			
	Thursday			
	Friday			
	Saturday			
	Sunday			

Notes

Quiz **31**

1 jurist	6 forbidden	11 constancy
2 demoralize	7 atypical	12 scientifically
3 windfall	8 masterful	13 billing
4 incidentally	9 nourishment	14 nicotine
5 vain	10 doctorate	15 pogrom

Not representative of a group, class, or type

With respect to science; in a scientific way

Excluded from use or mention

An alkaloid poison that occurs in tobacco; used in medicine and as an insecticide

Fruit that has fallen from the tree

Organized persecution of an ethnic group

Corrupt morally or by intemperance or sensuality

Introducing a different topic; in point of fact

The quality of being enduring and free from change or variation

Request for payment of a debt

Having or revealing supreme mastery or skill

One of the highest earned academic degrees conferred by a university

A legal scholar versed in civil law or the law of nations

What needs to be eaten to sustain a person's body; food containing the required vitamins and energy

Characteristic of false pride; having an exaggerated sense of self-importance

Week #_______ From ____/____/____ to ____/____/____

Date	Weekday	Morning	Afternoon	Evening
	Monday			
	Tuesday			
	Wednesday			
	Thursday			
	Friday			
	Saturday			
	Sunday			

Notes

1	cripple	6	mutation	11	impatience
2	terrestrial	7	disaffected	12	inexperienced
3	weighting	8	conjunction	13	mutuality
4	stereotyped	9	deacon	14	extra
5	amplifier	10	posting	15	mischief

- [ ] Lacking spontaneity, originality or individuality

- [ ] A Protestant layman who assists the minister

- [ ] A lack of patience; irritation with anything that causes delay

- [ ] More than is needed, desired, or required

- [ ] A reciprocal relation between interdependent entities

- [ ] Reckless or malicious behavior that causes discomfort or annoyance in others

- [ ] Of or relating to or inhabiting the land as opposed to the sea or air

- [ ] Deprive of strength or efficiency; make useless or worthless

- [ ] Lacking practical experience or training

- [ ] Discontented as toward authority

- [ ] Electronic equipment that increases strength of signals passing through it

- [ ] A sign posted in a public place as an advertisement

- [ ] A coefficient assigned to elements of a frequency distribution in order to represent their relative importance

- [ ] An organism that has characteristics resulting from chromosomal alteration

- [ ] The temporal property of two things happening at the same time

Week #_______ From _____/_____/_____   to _____/_____/_____

Date	Weekday	Morning	Afternoon	Evening
	Monday			
	Tuesday			
	Wednesday			
	Thursday			
	Friday			
	Saturday			
	Sunday			

Notes

1 handset	6 bottom	11 eloquence
2 brilliance	7 accompaniment	12 publicized
3 scourge	8 schism	13 opaque
4 camaraderie	9 underwater	14 reactionary
5 almighty	10 private	15 reconnaissance

☐ Powerful and effective language

☐ A light within the field of vision that is brighter than the brightness to which the eyes are adapted

☐ Not transmitting light or other radiation; impenetrable to sight

☐ An extreme conservative; an opponent of progress or liberalism

☐ Confined to particular persons, groups or providing privacy

☐ The quality of affording easy familiarity and sociability

☐ The act of scouting or exploring

☐ Beneath the surface of the water

☐ The lower side of anything

☐ An event or situation that happens at the same time as or in connection with another

☐ Division of a group into opposing factions

☐ Having unlimited power

☐ A whip used to inflict punishment

☐ Telephone set with the mouthpiece and earpiece mounted on a single handle

☐ Made known; especially made widely known

Week #_______ From _____/_____/_____ to _____/_____/_____

Date	Weekday	Morning	Afternoon	Evening
	Monday			
	Tuesday			
	Wednesday			
	Thursday			
	Friday			
	Saturday			
	Sunday			

Notes

1	yielding	6	stronghold	11	primordial
2	consulate	7	manifold	12	revert
3	rightist	8	unravel	13	sliding
4	demography	9	denote	14	headphone
5	alternation	10	manpower	15	nobility

- [ ] A strongly fortified defensive structure
- [ ] Being a smooth continuous motion
- [ ] Believing in or supporting tenets of the political right
- [ ] The branch of sociology that studies the characteristics of human populations
- [ ] Electro-acoustic transducer for converting electric signals into sounds; it is held over or inserted into the ear
- [ ] Become or cause to become undone by separating the fibers or threads of
- [ ] A privileged class holding hereditary titles
- [ ] Many and varied; having many features or forms
- [ ] Inclined to yield to argument, influence or control
- [ ] Diplomatic building that serves as the residence or workplace of a consul
- [ ] Successive change from one thing or state to another and back again
- [ ] Be a sign or indication of
- [ ] The force of workers available
- [ ] Go back to a previous state
- [ ] Having existed from the beginning; in an earliest or original stage or state

Week #______   From ____/____/____   to ____/____/____

Date	Weekday	Morning	Afternoon	Evening
	Monday			
	Tuesday			
	Wednesday			
	Thursday			
	Friday			
	Saturday			
	Sunday			

Notes

1 band	6 archetype	11 renter
2 nuance	7 tuning	12 supersede
3 homelessness	8 forage	13 wean
4 collateral	9 marginalize	14 sentient
5 impassioned	10 mite	15 nanotechnology

☐ The state or condition of having no home

☐ The branch of engineering that deals with things smaller than 100 nanometers

☐ A subtle difference in meaning, opinion or attitude

☐ Descended from a common ancestor but through different lines

☐ Bulky food like grass or hay for browsing or grazing horses or cattle

☐ Characterized by intense emotion

☐ An unofficial association of people or groups

☐ Someone who pays rent to use land or a building or a car that is owned by someone else

☐ Take the place or move into the position of

☐ Endowed with feeling and unstructured consciousness

☐ Gradually deprive of mother's milk

☐ Relegate to a lower or outer edge, as of specific groups of people

☐ A slight but appreciable amount

☐ To a standard frequency

☐ Something that serves as a model or a basis for making copies

Week #_______ From _____/_____/_____ to _____/_____/_____

Date	Weekday	Morning	Afternoon	Evening
	Monday			
	Tuesday			
	Wednesday			
	Thursday			
	Friday			
	Saturday			
	Sunday			

Notes

1	revisionist	6	subatomic	11	portraiture
2	spotty	7	chartered	12	submissive
3	zealot	8	insulting	13	utensil
4	fractious	9	overriding	14	warp
5	fortitude	10	teeming	15	misbehavior

☐ Inclined or willing to submit to orders or wishes of others or showing such inclination

☐ Having spots or patches

☐ Improper, wicked or immoral behavior

☐ Hired for the exclusive temporary use of a group of travelers

☐ A word picture of a person's appearance and character

☐ A fervent and even militant proponent of something

☐ Strength of mind that enables one to endure adversity with courage

☐ Of or relating to constituents of the atom or forces within the atom

☐ Stubbornly resistant to authority or control

☐ Abundantly filled with especially living things

☐ Expressing extreme contempt

☐ Having superior power and influence

☐ A Communist who tries to rewrite Marxism to justify a retreat from the revolutionary position

☐ Bend out of shape, as under pressure or from heat

☐ An implement for practical use

Week #_____ From ____/____/____ to ____/____/____

Date	Weekday	Morning	Afternoon	Evening
	Monday			
	Tuesday			
	Wednesday			
	Thursday			
	Friday			
	Saturday			
	Sunday			

Notes

1	hapless	6	converter	11	connotation
2	dispersed	7	vigilance	12	registrar
3	conservator	8	tightening	13	mechanized
4	reckless	9	deluxe	14	nascent
5	requisite	10	monopolize	15	unfinished

- [ ] Rich and superior in quality
- [ ] Distributed over a wide area
- [ ] The custodian of a collection
- [ ] Have and control fully and exclusively
- [ ] Deserving or inciting pity
- [ ] The process of paying close and continuous attention
- [ ] Necessary for relief or supply
- [ ] Equipped with machinery
- [ ] The act of making something tighter
- [ ] Someone responsible for keeping records
- [ ] Marked by defiant disregard for danger or consequences
- [ ] Not brought to the desired final state
- [ ] Being born or beginning
- [ ] What you must know in order to determine the reference of an expression
- [ ] A device for changing one substance, form or state into another

Week #_____ From ____/____/____ to ____/____/____

Date	Weekday	Morning	Afternoon	Evening
	Monday			
	Tuesday			
	Wednesday			
	Thursday			
	Friday			
	Saturday			
	Sunday			

Notes

1 fore	6 wimp	11 extraneous
2 methyl	7 cognizant	12 salient
3 stymie	8 glorification	13 figuration
4 chinook	9 orphaned	14 affliction
5 gothic	10 keyword	15 determining

☐ Representing figuratively as by emblem or allegory

☐ A state of high honor

☐ Not pertinent to the matter under consideration

☐ As if belonging to the Middle Ages; old-fashioned and unenlightened

☐ A situation in golf where an opponent's ball blocks the line between your ball and the hole

☐ Deprived of parents by death or desertion

☐ Situated at or toward the bow of a vessel

☐ A person who lacks confidence, is irresolute and wishy-washy

☐ Having the power or quality of deciding

☐ A word that is used as a pattern to decode an encrypted message

☐ The univalent radical CH3- derived from methane

☐ A warm dry wind blowing down the eastern slopes of the Rockies

☐ Having a quality that thrusts itself into attention

☐ Having or showing knowledge or understanding or realization or perception

☐ A state oaf great suffering and distress due to adversity

Week #_______ From _____/_____/_____   to _____/_____/_____

Date	Weekday	Morning	Afternoon	Evening
	Monday			
	Tuesday			
	Wednesday			
	Thursday			
	Friday			
	Saturday			
	Sunday			

Notes

1	turbulence	6	chronically	11	buyout
2	cornerstone	7	ballast	12	ardent
3	excursion	8	habitual	13	bibliography
4	bottleneck	9	hadron	14	childlike
5	idealize	10	nostalgic	15	tone

- [ ] Unhappy about being away and longing for familiar things or persons
- [ ] Acquisition of a company by purchasing a controlling percentage of its stock
- [ ] A narrowing that reduces the flow through a channel
- [ ] Any heavy material used to stabilize a ship or airship
- [ ] Befitting a young child
- [ ] The quality of a person's voice
- [ ] Commonly used or practiced; usual
- [ ] The fundamental assumptions from which something is begun, developed, calculated or explained
- [ ] Unstable flow of a liquid or gas
- [ ] A journey taken for pleasure
- [ ] Consider or render as ideal
- [ ] Any elementary particle that interacts strongly with other particles
- [ ] Characterized by intense emotion
- [ ] In a habitual and longstanding manner
- [ ] A list of writings with time and place of publication

Week #_____ From ____/____/____ to ____/____/____

Date	Weekday	Morning	Afternoon	Evening
	Monday			
	Tuesday			
	Wednesday			
	Thursday			
	Friday			
	Saturday			
	Sunday			

Notes

Quiz **40**

1 buoyant	6 arable	11 buoyancy
2 tantalizing	7 wasteland	12 exile
3 firewall	8 retinal	13 immortal
4 simulated	9 anarchic	14 excessively
5 enactment	10 conveyor	15 array

☐ An orderly arrangement

☐ In or relating to the retina of the eye

☐ Not genuine or real; being an imitation of the genuine article

☐ Expel from a country

☐ The passing of a law by a legislative body

☐ Not subject to death

☐ An uninhabited wilderness that is worthless for cultivation

☐ To a degree exceeding normal or proper limits

☐ Tending to float on a liquid or rise in air or gas

☐ Arousing desire or expectation for something unattainable or mockingly out of reach

☐ Capable of being farmed productively

☐ Cheerfulness that bubbles to the surface

☐ A person who conveys

☐ The application of maximum thrust

☐ Without law or control

Week #_____ From ____/____/____ to ____/____/____

Date	Weekday	Morning	Afternoon	Evening
	Monday			
	Tuesday			
	Wednesday			
	Thursday			
	Friday			
	Saturday			
	Sunday			

Notes

1 estimation	6 unchallenged	11 seeking
2 optics	7 mainframe	12 logistics
3 restate	8 desecration	13 testator
4 infantile	9 obstruct	14 earner
5 craving	10 adamant	15 caloric

☐ An intense desire for some particular thing

☐ Someone who earn wages in return for their labor

☐ Impervious to pleas, persuasion, requests, reason

☐ Generally agreed upon; not subject to dispute

☐ Blasphemous behavior; the act of depriving something of its sacred character

☐ The branch of physics that studies the physical properties of light

☐ A person who makes a will

☐ Indicating a lack of maturity

☐ Hinder or prevent the progress or accomplishment of

☐ A large digital computer serving 100-400 users and occupying a special air-conditioned room

☐ Management of the supplies and transport required for an operation

☐ The act of searching for something

☐ A document appraising the value of something

☐ To say, state, or perform again

☐ Relating to or associated with heat

Week #_____ From ____/____/____ to ____/____/____

Date	Weekday	Morning	Afternoon	Evening
	Monday			
	Tuesday			
	Wednesday			
	Thursday			
	Friday			
	Saturday			
	Sunday			

Notes

>

>

>

>

>

>

>

>

>

>

>

>

>

>

>

>

>

>

1 conciliation	6 mainstay	11 tightness
2 depravity	7 sprinkler	12 fend
3 suffrage	8 pique	13 impasse
4 contributing	9 uninterrupted	14 brothel
5 humankind	10 pathos	15 fodder

- [ ] A sudden outburst of anger
- [ ] Having undisturbed continuity
- [ ] A quality that arouses emotions
- [ ] A situation in which no progress can be made or no advancement is possible
- [ ] Try to manage without help
- [ ] The right to vote in political elections
- [ ] A prominent supporter
- [ ] All of the living human inhabitants of the earth
- [ ] Mechanical device that attaches to a garden hose for watering lawn or garden
- [ ] Tending to bring about; being partly responsible for
- [ ] The state of manifesting goodwill and cooperation after being reconciled
- [ ] A state occasioned by scarcity of money and a shortage of credit
- [ ] Soldiers who are regarded as expendable in the face of artillery fire
- [ ] A building where prostitutes are available
- [ ] Moral perversion; impairment of virtue and moral principles

Week #_______ From _____/_____/_____ to _____/_____/_____

Date	Weekday	Morning	Afternoon	Evening
	Monday			
	Tuesday			
	Wednesday			
	Thursday			
	Friday			
	Saturday			
	Sunday			

Notes

1 confined	6 stratum	11 unsuitable
2 profile	7 biceps	12 itinerant
3 incarnation	8 intuitive	13 handicap
4 tempting	9 embellish	14 disinterest
5 ploy	10 earthbound	15 reformed

☐ Make appear better or greater than reality

☐ An analysis representing the extent to which something exhibits various characteristics

☐ Not meant or adapted for a particular purpose

☐ Tolerance attributable to a lack of involvement

☐ Travelling from place to place to work

☐ Highly attractive and able to arouse hope or desire

☐ Spontaneously derived from or prompted by a natural tendency

☐ Confined to the earth

☐ One of several parallel layers of material arranged one on top of another

☐ Caused to abandon an evil manner of living and follow a good one

☐ A new personification of a familiar idea

☐ Any skeletal muscle having two origins

☐ Not free to move about

☐ The condition of being unable to perform as a consequence of physical or mental unfitness

☐ A tactic or maneuver intended to gain an advantage

Week #_______ From _____/_____/_____ to _____/_____/_____

Date	Weekday	Morning	Afternoon	Evening
	Monday			
	Tuesday			
	Wednesday			
	Thursday			
	Friday			
	Saturday			
	Sunday			

Notes

1 stag	6 polarization	11 noxious
2 garb	7 captivity	12 autocratic
3 mismatch	8 changed	13 confound
4 despise	9 quirk	14 companionship
5 gunner	10 millimeter	15 landscape

☐ Made or become different in nature or form

☐ The state of being with someone

☐ The phenomenon in which waves of light or other radiation are restricted in direction of vibration

☐ A bad or unsuitable match

☐ The state of being imprisoned

☐ Clothing of a distinctive style or for a particular occasion

☐ Injurious to physical or mental health

☐ Be confusing or perplexing to; cause to be unable to think clearly

☐ A male deer, especially an adult male red deer

☐ Offensively self-assured or given to exercising usually unwarranted power

☐ Look down on with disdain

☐ A serviceman in the artillery

☐ A strange attitude or habit

☐ A metric unit of length equal to one thousandth of a meter

☐ An expanse of scenery that can be seen in a single view

Week #_______ From _____/_____/_____ to _____/_____/_____

Date	Weekday	Morning	Afternoon	Evening
	Monday			
	Tuesday			
	Wednesday			
	Thursday			
	Friday			
	Saturday			
	Sunday			

Notes

1 tenderness	6 savior	11 accessibility
2 ordained	7 festivity	12 sharing
3 proficiency	8 saloon	13 coercion
4 xenophobia	9 duress	14 interceptor
5 starry	10 slurry	15 hacker

☐ Fixed or established especially by order or command

☐ A room or establishment where alcoholic drinks are served over a counter

☐ Compulsory force or threat

☐ The quality of being at hand when needed

☐ The quality of having great facility and competence

☐ The act of compelling by force of authority

☐ A suspension of insoluble particles usually in water

☐ A person who rescues you from harm or danger

☐ Unselfishly willing to share with others

☐ A fast maneuverable fighter plane designed to intercept enemy aircraft

☐ A tendency to express warm and affectionate feeling

☐ Any joyous diversion

☐ Abounding with or resembling stars

☐ A fear of foreigners or strangers

☐ Someone who plays golf poorly

Week #_______ From _____/_____/_____ to _____/_____/_____

Date	Weekday	Morning	Afternoon	Evening
	Monday			
	Tuesday			
	Wednesday			
	Thursday			
	Friday			
	Saturday			
	Sunday			

Notes

1 delve	6 signatory	11 recourse
2 coronation	7 synchronous	12 inept
3 mantra	8 invalid	13 provost
4 oppressive	9 heinous	14 exorbitant
5 prohibitive	10 perpendicular	15 forged

☐ The ceremony of installing a new monarch

☐ Occurring or existing at the same time or having the same period or phase

☐ A high-ranking university administrator

☐ Reproduced fraudulently

☐ Act of turning to for assistance

☐ Someone who is incapacitated by a chronic illness or injury

☐ Extremely wicked, deeply criminal

☐ Tending to discourage

☐ Turn up, loosen, or remove earth

☐ Intersecting at or forming right angles

☐ Weighing heavily on the senses or spirit

☐ Someone who signs and is bound by a document

☐ Not elegant or graceful in expression

☐ Greatly exceeding bounds of reason or moderation

☐ A commonly repeated word or phrase

Week #_______ From ____/____/____ to ____/____/____

Date	Weekday	Morning	Afternoon	Evening
	Monday			
	Tuesday			
	Wednesday			
	Thursday			
	Friday			
	Saturday			
	Sunday			

Notes

1 shipyard	6 meager	11 entrant
2 reflex	7 tarnish	12 diversification
3 scrupulous	8 uncanny	13 unnamed
4 leakage	9 cogent	14 flexor
5 otherworldly	10 militiaman	15 banality

☐ A skeletal muscle whose contraction bends a joint

☐ A workplace where ships are built or repaired

☐ Deficient in amount, quality or extent

☐ A member of the militia; serves only during emergencies

☐ A commodity that enters competition with established merchandise

☐ The act of introducing variety

☐ A trite or obvious remark

☐ Powerfully persuasive

☐ Make dirty or spotty, as by exposure to air; also used metaphorically

☐ An automatic instinctive unlearned reaction to a stimulus

☐ Having scruples; arising from a sense of right and wrong; principled

☐ Existing outside of or not in accordance with nature

☐ Being or having a source that is not known or who's name is unknown

☐ The discharge of a fluid from some container

☐ Suggesting the operation of supernatural influences

Week #_______ From ______/______/______   to ______/______/______

Date	Weekday	Morning	Afternoon	Evening
	Monday			
	Tuesday			
	Wednesday			
	Thursday			
	Friday			
	Saturday			
	Sunday			

Notes

1	aerobic	6	hyperactive	11	dated
2	seeming	7	bode	12	facilitator
3	glaucoma	8	inland	13	privy
4	bounty	9	declarative	14	weld
5	shifter	10	vale	15	musket

☐ For acts such as catching criminals or killing predatory animals or enlisting in the military

☐ A muzzle-loading shoulder gun with a long barrel; formerly used by infantrymen

☐ A stagehand responsible for moving scenery

☐ An outdoor building with an (often primitive) toilet

☐ An eye disease that damages the optic nerve and impairs vision

☐ Someone who makes progress easier

☐ Situated away from an area's coast or border

☐ Depending on free oxygen or air

☐ Appearing as such but not necessarily so

☐ A long depression in the surface of the land that usually contains a river

☐ Marked by features of the immediate and usually discounted past

☐ Relating to the use of or having the nature of a declaration

☐ Join together by heating

☐ More active than normal

☐ Be a sign of something to come, especially something important or bad

Week #_____ From ____/____/____ to ____/____/____

Date	Weekday	Morning	Afternoon	Evening
	Monday			
	Tuesday			
	Wednesday			
	Thursday			
	Friday			
	Saturday			
	Sunday			

Notes

1	burrow	6	hyperbole	11	ascetic
2	intermarriage	7	creeping	12	revoke
3	multiplicity	8	lavish	13	surveyor
4	harbinger	9	fortify	14	tandem
5	topography	10	pauper	15	material

- [ ] Marriage to a person belonging to a tribe or group other than your own as required by custom or law

- [ ] The property of being multiple

- [ ] The mistake of not following suit when able to do so

- [ ] Something that precedes and indicates the approach of something or someone

- [ ] The configuration of a surface and the relations among its man-made and natural features

- [ ] Practicing great self-denial

- [ ] A hole made by an animal, usually for shelter

- [ ] A slow mode of locomotion on hands and knees or dragging the body

- [ ] An arrangement of two or more objects or persons one behind another

- [ ] Extravagant exaggeration

- [ ] The tangible substance that goes into the makeup of a physical object

- [ ] Expend profusely; also used with abstract nouns

- [ ] Make strong or stronger

- [ ] A person who is very poor

- [ ] An engineer who determines the boundaries and elevations of land or structures

Week #_______ From _____/_____/_____ to _____/_____/_____

Date	Weekday	Morning	Afternoon	Evening
	Monday			
	Tuesday			
	Wednesday			
	Thursday			
	Friday			
	Saturday			
	Sunday			

Notes

1 prey	6 anesthesia	11 midway
2 newsgroup	7 embellishment	12 sheltered
3 otolaryngology	8 vile	13 groom
4 utterance	9 persevere	14 polygamy
5 incubation	10 illustrious	15 miscellaneous

☐ Protected from danger or bad weather

☐ Elaboration of an interpretation by the use of decorative detail

☐ Having more than one spouse at a time

☐ Consisting of a haphazard assortment of different kinds

☐ Educate for a future role or function

☐ The use of uttered sounds for auditory communication

☐ Morally reprehensible

☐ Loss of bodily sensation with or without loss of consciousness

☐ Equally distant from the extremes

☐ Be persistent, refuse to stop

☐ Widely known and esteemed

☐ Maintaining something at the most favorable temperature for its development

☐ The medical specialty that deals with diseases of the ear, nose and throat

☐ A collection of messages about a particular topic accessed over the Internet

☐ A person who is the aim of an attack by some hostile person or influence

Week #______ From ____/____/____ to ____/____/____

Date	Weekday	Morning	Afternoon	Evening
	Monday			
	Tuesday			
	Wednesday			
	Thursday			
	Friday			
	Saturday			
	Sunday			

Notes

Quiz **51**

1 enjoyable	6 precarious	11 rainfall
2 idolatry	7 preventable	12 arcade
3 sentinel	8 ghetto	13 afflicted
4 unfounded	9 flora	14 rejoinder
5 fungicide	10 paleontology	15 rebuff

- [ ] The earth science that studies fossil organisms and related remains

- [ ] Any agent that destroys or prevents the growth of fungi

- [ ] Religious zeal; the willingness to serve God

- [ ] A quick reply to a question or remark

- [ ] Without a basis in reason or fact

- [ ] Water falling in drops from vapor condensed in the atmosphere

- [ ] A covered passageway with shops and stalls on either side

- [ ] Grievously affected especially by disease

- [ ] Capable of being prevented

- [ ] Formerly the restricted quarter of many European cities in which Jews were required to live

- [ ] A person employed to keep watch for some anticipated event

- [ ] All the plant life in a particular region or period

- [ ] Affording satisfaction or pleasure

- [ ] Reject outright and bluntly

- [ ] Affording no ease or reassurance

Week #_______ From ____/____/_____   to ____/____/_____

Date	Weekday	Morning	Afternoon	Evening
	Monday			
	Tuesday			
	Wednesday			
	Thursday			
	Friday			
	Saturday			
	Sunday			

Notes

➤
➤
➤
➤
➤
➤
➤
➤
➤
➤
➤
➤
➤
➤
➤
➤
➤
➤
➤

1 pundit	6 shyness	11 messianic
2 fable	7 usurp	12 inactive
3 commodore	8 regroup	13 exact
4 forebear	9 unfriendly	14 ascending
5 domestication	10 tether	15 shepherd

- [ ] An expert or critic in a particular field who often presents their views to the media

- [ ] Adaptation to intimate association with human beings

- [ ] Organize anew, as after a setback

- [ ] A commissioned naval officer who ranks above a captain and below a rear admiral; the lowest grade of admiral

- [ ] A person from whom you are descended

- [ ] Marked by strict and particular and complete accordance with fact

- [ ] A deliberately false or improbable account

- [ ] A clergyman who watches over a group of people

- [ ] A feeling of fear of embarrassment

- [ ] Not easy to understand or use

- [ ] Take control of; take as one's right or possession

- [ ] Moving, going or growing upward

- [ ] Of or relating to a messiah promising deliverance

- [ ] Restraint consisting of a rope (or light chain) used to restrain an animal

- [ ] Lacking activity; lying idle or unused

Week #_____ From ____/____/____ to ____/____/____

Date	Weekday	Morning	Afternoon	Evening
	Monday			
	Tuesday			
	Wednesday			
	Thursday			
	Friday			
	Saturday			
	Sunday			

Notes

>
>
>
>
>
>
>
>
>
>
>
>
>
>
>
>
>
>
>
>
>

1	undersea	6	launcher	11	jogging
2	traveling	7	hypocrisy	12	importation
3	pathologist	8	panoply	13	hauler
4	panacea	9	spillover	14	louse
5	fervent	10	keystone	15	culmination

☐ A haulage contractor

☐ Running at a jog trot as a form of cardiopulmonary exercise

☐ The commercial activity of buying and bringing in goods from a foreign country

☐ Armament in the form of a device capable of launching a rocket

☐ An expression of agreement that is not supported by real conviction

☐ Hypothetical remedy for all ills or diseases; once sought by the alchemists

☐ A complete and impressive array

☐ The act of going from one place to another

☐ A central cohesive source of support and stability

☐ Characterized by intense emotion

☐ Wingless usually flattened bloodsucking insect parasitic on warm-blooded animals

☐ Beneath the surface of the sea

☐ A doctor who specializes in medical diagnosis

☐ A final climactic stage

☐ Any indirect effect of public expenditure

Week #_____ From ____/____/____ to ____/____/____

Date	Weekday	Morning	Afternoon	Evening
	Monday			
	Tuesday			
	Wednesday			
	Thursday			
	Friday			
	Saturday			
	Sunday			

Notes

Quiz 54

1	insistent	6	prosthesis	11	biased
2	denomination	7	seamless	12	rotor
3	invigorating	8	naturalist	13	blanket
4	disparaging	9	perpetuation	14	chromium
5	typing	10	excavate	15	philanthropic

- [ ] Generous in assistance to the poor
- [ ] Repetitive and persistent
- [ ] Favoring one person or side over another
- [ ] Corrective consisting of a replacement for a part of the body
- [ ] Recover through digging
- [ ] A group of religious congregations having its own organization and a distinctive faith
- [ ] Writing done with a typewriter
- [ ] A hard brittle multivalent metallic element; resistant to corrosion and tarnishing
- [ ] An advocate of the doctrine that the world can be understood in scientific terms
- [ ] The act of prolonging something
- [ ] Not having or joined by a seam or seams
- [ ] The rotating armature of a motor or generator
- [ ] Expressive of low opinion
- [ ] Imparting strength and vitality
- [ ] Bedding that keeps a person warm in bed

Week #_______ From ____/____/____ to ____/____/____

Date	Weekday	Morning	Afternoon	Evening
	Monday			
	Tuesday			
	Wednesday			
	Thursday			
	Friday			
	Saturday			
	Sunday			

Notes

➤

➤

➤

➤

➤

➤

➤

➤

➤

➤

➤

➤

➤

➤

➤

➤

➤

➤

1	borderline	6	transformed	11	rationality
2	bleach	7	uneasiness	12	rallying
3	intifada	8	stabilizing	13	impervious
4	bearer	9	primal	14	pious
5	scrap	10	offshoot	15	remedy

- [ ] Given a completely different form or appearance

- [ ] Of questionable or minimal quality

- [ ] A small fragment of something broken off from the whole

- [ ] The act of mobilizing for a common purpose

- [ ] Causing to become stable

- [ ] Serving as an essential component

- [ ] Not admitting of passage or capable of being affected

- [ ] Having, showing or expressing reverence for a deity

- [ ] The state of having good sense and sound judgment

- [ ] The whiteness that results from removing the color from something

- [ ] Feelings of anxiety that make you tense and irritable

- [ ] A natural consequence of development

- [ ] Act of correcting an error or a fault or an evil

- [ ] An uprising by Palestinian Arabs against Israel in the late 1980s and again in 2000

- [ ] Someone whose employment involves carrying something

Week #_______ From ____/____/____   to ____/____/____

Date	Weekday	Morning	Afternoon	Evening
	Monday			
	Tuesday			
	Wednesday			
	Thursday			
	Friday			
	Saturday			
	Sunday			

Notes

➢
➢
➢
➢
➢
➢
➢
➢
➢
➢
➢
➢
➢
➢
➢
➢
➢
➢

Quiz 56

1	vigilant	6	baptism	11	lamentation
2	endlessly	7	pharaoh	12	synonym
3	internment	8	bioscience	13	refurbish
4	lyric	9	suffuse	14	consumerism
5	defenseless	10	tuber	15	copier

☐ The theory that an increasing consumption of goods is economically beneficial

☐ Continuing forever without end

☐ A fleshy underground stem or root serving for reproductive and food storage

☐ Small red ant of warm regions; a common household pest

☐ Any of the branches of natural science dealing with the structure and behavior of living organisms

☐ The text of a popular song or musical-comedy number

☐ A Christian sacrament signifying spiritual cleansing and rebirth

☐ A cry of sorrow and grief

☐ Cause to spread or flush or flood through, over, or across

☐ Lacking protection or support

☐ Redecorate and brighten up to make nicer for inhabiting and/or use

☐ Two words that can be interchanged in a context are said to be synonymous relative to that context

☐ Apparatus that makes copies of typed, written or drawn material

☐ Confinement during wartime

☐ Carefully observant or attentive; on the lookout for possible danger

Week #_______ From ____/____/____ to ____/____/____

Date	Weekday	Morning	Afternoon	Evening
	Monday			
	Tuesday			
	Wednesday			
	Thursday			
	Friday			
	Saturday			
	Sunday			

Notes

Quiz **57**

1	nemesis	6	acknowledged	11	strident
2	vulture	7	flowing	12	raise
3	infancy	8	matron	13	lastly
4	quintessential	9	catechism	14	provocation
5	bison	10	stasis	15	outlying

☐ Increase the level or amount of something

☐ Any of several large humped bovids having shaggy manes and large heads and short horns

☐ Any of various large diurnal birds of prey having naked heads and weak claws and feeding chiefly on carrion

☐ Unfriendly behavior that causes anger or resentment

☐ A married woman who is staid and dignified

☐ An abnormal state in which the normal flow of a liquid is slowed or stopped

☐ A series of questions put to an individual to elicit their views

☐ Recognized or made known or admitted

☐ The motion characteristic of fluids

☐ The early stage of growth or development

☐ Relatively far from a center or middle

☐ Conspicuously and offensively loud; given to vehement outcry

☐ Representing the perfect example of a class or quality

☐ Introducing the last item or a series

☐ Something causing misery or death

Week #______ From ____/____/____ to ____/____/____

Date	Weekday	Morning	Afternoon	Evening
	Monday			
	Tuesday			
	Wednesday			
	Thursday			
	Friday			
	Saturday			
	Sunday			

Notes

1 stockholder	6 fang	11 pedigree
2 insular	7 exalted	12 attendant
3 pretense	8 neurotic	13 compulsion
4 fostering	9 overuse	14 diatribe
5 discontent	10 handiwork	15 vandalism

☐ An appendage of insects that is capable of injecting venom; usually evolved from the legs

☐ The descendants of one individual

☐ Characteristic of or affected by neurosis

☐ Someone who waits on or attends to the needs of another

☐ Thunderous verbal attack

☐ Encouragement; aiding the development of something

☐ A work produced by hand labor

☐ Of high moral or intellectual value; elevated in nature or style

☐ An urge to do or say something that might be better left undone or unsaid

☐ Deliberate destruction, defacement or damage of public or other people's property

☐ The act of giving a false appearance

☐ Relating to or characteristic of or situated on an island

☐ A longing for something better than the present situation

☐ Someone who holds shares of stock in a corporation

☐ Exploitation to the point of diminishing returns

Week #_______ From _____/_____/_____ to _____/_____/_____

Date	Weekday	Morning	Afternoon	Evening
	Monday			
	Tuesday			
	Wednesday			
	Thursday			
	Friday			
	Saturday			
	Sunday			

Notes

1	memorization	6	redeem	11	liable
2	extol	7	ephemeral	12	sharecropper
3	mead	8	deference	13	visceral
4	admonition	9	emitter	14	degeneration
5	vortex	10	flank	15	infantryman

☐ The electrode in a transistor where electrons originate

☐ Lasting a very short time

☐ Praise, glorify, or honor

☐ Made of fermented honey and water

☐ The process of declining from a higher to a lower level of effective power, vitality or essential quality

☐ Cautionary advice about something imminent

☐ Be located at the sides of something or somebody

☐ The shape of something rotating rapidly

☐ At risk of or subject to experiencing something usually unpleasant

☐ Fights on foot with small arms

☐ Prevent committing sins

☐ A courteous expression of esteem or regard

☐ Learning so as to be able to remember verbatim

☐ Small farmers and tenants

☐ Relating to or affecting the viscera

Week #_____ From ____/____/____ to ____/____/____

Date	Weekday	Morning	Afternoon	Evening
	Monday			
	Tuesday			
	Wednesday			
	Thursday			
	Friday			
	Saturday			
	Sunday			

Notes

1	noticeable	6	crux	11	gamma
2	photovoltaic	7	carotene	12	brainstorming
3	nonsensical	8	polluted	13	burr
4	authorship	9	tumultuous	14	abused
5	exploited	10	cordial	15	interlude

- [ ] Rendered unwholesome by contaminants and pollution
- [ ] The act of creating written works
- [ ] An intervening period or episode
- [ ] Developed or used to greatest advantage
- [ ] Seed vessel having hooks or prickles
- [ ] A group problem-solving technique in which members spontaneously share ideas and solutions
- [ ] Incongruous; inviting ridicule
- [ ] Characterized by unrest, disorder or insubordination
- [ ] Used improperly or excessively especially drugs
- [ ] The 3rd letter of the Greek alphabet
- [ ] An orange isomer of an unsaturated hydrocarbon found in many plants; is converted into vitamin A in the liver
- [ ] Capable or worthy of being perceived
- [ ] Diffusing warmth and friendliness
- [ ] Producing a voltage when exposed to radiant energy
- [ ] The most important point

Week #_____ From ____/____/____ to ____/____/____

Date	Weekday	Morning	Afternoon	Evening
	Monday			
	Tuesday			
	Wednesday			
	Thursday			
	Friday			
	Saturday			
	Sunday			

Notes

1 wand	6 inhibitor	11 sorcery
2 debilitating	7 sandwich	12 stealth
3 rebuttal	8 tribesman	13 snap
4 clock	9 preserved	14 durability
5 disposable	10 lobe	15 substandard

Impairing the strength and vitality

Prevented from decaying or spoiling and prepared for future use

A somewhat rounded subdivision of a bodily organ or part

Falling short of some prescribed norm

The belief in magical spells that harness occult forces or evil spirits to produce unnatural effects in the world

Permanence by virtue of the power to resist stress or force

Someone who lives in a tribe

The speech act of refuting by offering a contrary contention or argument

Avoiding detection by moving carefully

A substance that retards or stops an activity

A timepiece that shows the time of day

Utter in an angry, sharp, or abrupt tone

Free or available for use or disposition

Two slices of bread with a filling between them

A rod used by a magician or water diviner

Week #______ From ____/____/____ to ____/____/____

Date	Weekday	Morning	Afternoon	Evening
	Monday			
	Tuesday			
	Wednesday			
	Thursday			
	Friday			
	Saturday			
	Sunday			

Notes

1	tonality	6	impediment	11	symmetry
2	mediocre	7	boot	12	dearly
3	throttle	8	connectivity	13	agreeable
4	dogma	9	cadre	14	scanning
5	unionization	10	scriptural	15	obliterate

☐ In a sincere and heartfelt manner

☐ The process of translating photographs into a digital form that can be recognized by a computer

☐ Conforming to your own liking, feelings or nature

☐ A religious doctrine that is proclaimed as true without proof

☐ Something that interferes with action or progress

☐ The property of being connected or the degree to which something has connections

☐ Act of forming labor unions

☐ Mark for deletion, rub off, or erase

☐ Of or pertaining to or contained in or in accordance with the Bible

☐ An attribute of a shape or relation; exact reflection of form on opposite sides of a dividing line or plane

☐ A small unit serving as part of or as the nucleus of a larger political movement

☐ Any of 24 major or minor diatonic scales that provide the tonal framework for a piece of music

☐ A valve that regulates the supply of fuel to the engine

☐ Moderate to inferior in quality

☐ Footwear that covers the whole foot and lower leg

Week #_______ From _____/_____/_____ to _____/_____/_____

Date	Weekday	Morning	Afternoon	Evening
	Monday			
	Tuesday			
	Wednesday			
	Thursday			
	Friday			
	Saturday			
	Sunday			

Notes

1 masking	6 browse	11 Insatiable
2 scribe	7 fledgling	12 reschedule
3 oriented	8 messiah	13 metropolis
4 solicitation	9 dictation	14 diversified
5 alienated	10 equalization	15 yardstick

☐ Adjusted or located in relation to surroundings or circumstances; sometimes used in combination

☐ Socially disoriented

☐ Any expected deliverer

☐ Score a line on with a pointed instrument, as in metalworking

☐ Impossible to satisfy

☐ Assign a new time and place for an event

☐ A measure or standard used for comparison

☐ The act of making equal or uniform

☐ Vegetation that is suitable for animals to eat

☐ A large and densely populated urban area; may include several independent administrative districts

☐ Having variety of character or form or components; or having increased variety

☐ Having acquired its flight feathers

☐ The act of concealing the existence of something by obstructing the view of it

☐ An authoritative direction or instruction to do something

☐ An entreaty addressed to someone of superior status

Week #_____ From ____/____/____ to ____/____/____

Date	Weekday	Morning	Afternoon	Evening
	Monday			
	Tuesday			
	Wednesday			
	Thursday			
	Friday			
	Saturday			
	Sunday			

Notes

1	swine	6	puritan	11	refinement
2	deviate	7	destroyer	12	inspiring
3	trafficker	8	comparatively	13	desegregation
4	fell	9	saver	14	ophthalmologist
5	volition	10	agnostic	15	convert

☐ Someone who is doubtful or noncommittal about something

☐ Cause to fall by or as if by delivering a blow

☐ A medical doctor specializing in the diagnosis and treatment of diseases of the eye

☐ Turn aside; turn away from

☐ The capability of conscious choice and decision and intention

☐ Change from one system to another or to a new plan or policy

☐ Stout-bodied short-legged omnivorous animals

☐ The action of incorporating a racial or religious group into a community

☐ Someone who adheres to strict religious principles; someone opposed to sensual pleasures

☐ A highly developed state of perfection; having a flawless or impeccable quality

☐ Stimulating or exalting to the spirit

☐ A small fast lightly armored but heavily armed warship

☐ Someone who saves something from danger or violence

☐ In a relative manner; by comparison to something else

☐ Someone who promotes or exchanges goods or services for money

Week #_______ From ____/____/____ to ____/____/____

Date	Weekday	Morning	Afternoon	Evening
	Monday			
	Tuesday			
	Wednesday			
	Thursday			
	Friday			
	Saturday			
	Sunday			

Notes

1	originality	6	forestall	11	dismantling
2	bundled	7	commanding	8	evangelist
3	consign	8	pollination	13	close
4	stow	9	achievable	14	palisade
5	overlapping	10	methane	15	transatlantic

☐ Used of a height or viewpoint

☐ Keep from happening or arising; make impossible

☐ The ability to think and act independently

☐ A term to describe software that is sold together with hardware or other software

☐ Fill by packing tightly

☐ Move so that an opening or passage is obstructed; make shut

☐ Capable of existing or taking place or proving true; possible to do

☐ A preacher of the Christian gospel

☐ Fortification consisting of a strong fence made of stakes driven into the ground

☐ Crossing the Atlantic Ocean

☐ Commit forever; commit irrevocably

☐ A colorless odorless gas used as a fuel

☐ Transfer of pollen from the anther to the stigma of a plant

☐ The act of taking something apart

☐ Covering with a design in which one element covers a part of another

Week #_______ From _____/_____/_____   to _____/_____/_____

Date	Weekday	Morning	Afternoon	Evening
	Monday			
	Tuesday			
	Wednesday			
	Thursday			
	Friday			
	Saturday			
	Sunday			

Notes

➢
➢
➢
➢
➢
➢
➢
➢
➢
➢
➢
➢
➢
➢
➢
➢
➢
➢
➢

1	hostel	6	centimeter	11	lucid
2	implosion	7	nominal	12	rugby
3	layer	8	escalation	13	saber
4	gusto	9	superstition	14	coeducational
5	pride	10	usability	15	insomnia

☐ An increase, especially to counteract competition or aggression

☐ A sudden inward collapse

☐ A hotel providing overnight lodging for travelers

☐ A feeling of self-respect and personal worth

☐ Attended by members of both sexes

☐ Vigorous and enthusiastic enjoyment

☐ An irrational belief arising from ignorance or fear

☐ A form of football played with an oval ball

☐ An inability to sleep; chronic sleeplessness

☐ The quality of being able to provide good service

☐ A metric unit of length equal to one hundredth of a meter

☐ Relating to, constituting, bearing or giving a name

☐ Transparently clear; easily clear; easily understandable

☐ A fencing sword with a v-shaped blade and a slightly curved handle

☐ Single thickness of usually some homogeneous substance

Week #______ From ____/____/____ to ____/____/____

Date	Weekday	Morning	Afternoon	Evening
	Monday			
	Tuesday			
	Wednesday			
	Thursday			
	Friday			
	Saturday			
	Sunday			

Notes

1	vane	6	admonish	11	staggering
2	mouthpiece	7	booklet	12	totality
3	ingestion	8	bereft	13	fluency
4	genus	9	idiosyncrasy	14	adapted
5	perfectionist	10	squire	15	microbe

☐ A general kind of something

☐ A behavioral attribute that is distinctive and peculiar to an individual

☐ A minute life form; the term is not in technical use

☐ Unhappy in love; suffering from unrequited love

☐ Mechanical device attached to an elevated structure; rotates freely to show the direction of the wind

☐ Reprimand; express disapproval

☐ A part that goes over or into the mouth of a person

☐ Changed in order to improve or made more fit for a particular purpose

☐ So surprisingly impressive as to stun or overwhelm

☐ Young nobleman attendant on a knight

☐ Powerful and effective language

☐ The process of taking food into the body through the mouth

☐ A person who is displeased by anything that does not meet very high standards

☐ A small book usually having a paper cover

☐ The state of being total and complete

Week #______ From ____/____/____   to ____/____/____

Date	Weekday	Morning	Afternoon	Evening
	Monday			
	Tuesday			
	Wednesday			
	Thursday			
	Friday			
	Saturday			
	Sunday			

Notes

1 chaplain	6 rift	11 minefield
2 shortfall	7 abbey	12 burden
3 aversion	8 tempest	13 twain
4 polyp	9 eyewitness	14 distaste
5 handout	10 estrangement	15 spreading

☐ A spectator who can describe what happened

☐ A region in which explosives mines have been placed

☐ Process or result of distributing or extending over a wide expanse of space

☐ An onerous or difficult concern

☐ An announcement distributed to members of the press in order to supplement or replace an oral presentation

☐ The amount by which something is less than expected or required

☐ Separation resulting from hostility

☐ A violent commotion or disturbance

☐ A small vascular growth on the surface of a mucous membrane

☐ A feeling of intense dislike

☐ Two items of the same kind

☐ A clergyman ministering to some institution

☐ A gap between cloud masses

☐ A church associated with a monastery or convent

☐ A feeling of intense dislike

Week #_______ From ____/____/____ to ____/____/____

Date	Weekday	Morning	Afternoon	Evening
	Monday			
	Tuesday			
	Wednesday			
	Thursday			
	Friday			
	Saturday			
	Sunday			

Notes

1 testimonial	6 impaired	11 commensurate
2 embroidery	7 censor	12 accretion
3 edict	8 overestimate	13 beset
4 tailored	9 unwarranted	14 prerequisite
5 archetypal	10 offshore	15 reposition

☐ Make too high an estimate of

☐ Diminished in strength, quality, or utility

☐ An increase by natural growth or addition

☐ Something that serves as evidence

☐ A formal or authoritative proclamation

☐ Representing or constituting an original type after which other similar things are patterned

☐ Someone who censures or condemns

☐ Corresponding in size, degree or extent

☐ Something that is required in advance

☐ Annoy continually or chronically

☐ Depositing in a warehouse

☐ Away from shore; away from land

☐ Incapable of being justified or explained

☐ Adjust to a specific need or market

☐ Elaboration of an interpretation by the use of decorative detail

Week #_______ From ____/____/____ to ____/____/____

Date	Weekday	Morning	Afternoon	Evening
	Monday			
	Tuesday			
	Wednesday			
	Thursday			
	Friday			
	Saturday			
	Sunday			

Notes

1 evaluator	6 grocer	11 utopian
2 bioethics	7 utilitarian	12 revived
3 collaborator	8 leftist	13 acorn
4 prepaid	9 exhaustive	14 evocative
5 cubism	10 courtship	15 malfunction

- [ ] The branch of ethics that studies moral values in the biomedical sciences

- [ ] Serving to bring to mind

- [ ] Of or pertaining to or resembling a utopia

- [ ] A failure to function normally

- [ ] Fruit of the oak tree: a smooth thin-walled nut in a woody cup-shaped base

- [ ] Able to function usefully

- [ ] An authority who is able to estimate worth or quality

- [ ] A man's courting of a woman; seeking the affections of a woman

- [ ] Restored to consciousness, life or vigor

- [ ] Used especially of mail; paid in advance

- [ ] Someone who assists in a plot

- [ ] Believing in or supporting tenets of the political left

- [ ] A retail merchant who sells foodstuffs

- [ ] An artistic movement in France beginning in 1907 that featured surfaces of geometrical planes

- [ ] Performed comprehensively and completely

Week #_____ From ____/____/____ to ____/____/____

Date	Weekday	Morning	Afternoon	Evening
	Monday			
	Tuesday			
	Wednesday			
	Thursday			
	Friday			
	Saturday			
	Sunday			

Notes

➤
➤
➤
➤
➤
➤
➤
➤
➤
➤
➤
➤
➤
➤
➤
➤
➤
➤
➤

1	boiler	6	irreverent	11	mating
2	pronoun	7	benefactor	12	recuperation
3	eyesight	8	veracity	13	denigrate
4	plankton	9	teasing	14	footing
5	allotment	10	extremity	15	helplessness

- [ ] An external body part that projects from the body
- [ ] A device that heats water by burning fuel for use in a heating system
- [ ] Powerlessness revealed by an inability to act
- [ ] The aggregate of small plant and animal organisms that float or drift in great numbers in fresh or salt water
- [ ] A function word that is used in place of a noun or noun phrase
- [ ] Showing lack of due respect or veneration
- [ ] Status with respect to the relations between people or groups
- [ ] The act of harassing someone playfully or maliciously; provoking someone with persistent annoyances
- [ ] A person who helps people or institutions
- [ ] A share set aside for a specific purpose
- [ ] The quality of being truthful
- [ ] Gradual healing after sickness or injury
- [ ] Normal use of the faculty of vision
- [ ] The act of pairing a male and female for reproductive purposes
- [ ] Cause to seem less serious; play down

Week #_____ From ____/____/____ to ____/____/____

Date	Weekday	Morning	Afternoon	Evening
	Monday			
	Tuesday			
	Wednesday			
	Thursday			
	Friday			
	Saturday			
	Sunday			

Notes

1 misreading	6 oceanic	11 dwarf
2 bylaw	7 beaded	12 idiom
3 hamstring	8 discernment	13 cathode
4 hospitalize	9 ream	14 massacre
5 scathing	10 garner	15 platelet

☐ Marked by harshly abusive criticism

☐ A negatively charged electrode that is the source of electrons entering an electrical device

☐ Relating to or occurring or living in or frequenting the open ocean

☐ The cognitive condition of someone who understands

☐ A large quantity of written matter

☐ A manner of speaking that is natural to native speakers of a language

☐ Kill a large number of people indiscriminately

☐ A rule adopted by an organization in order to regulate its own affairs and the behavior of its members

☐ Admit into a hospital

☐ Misinterpretation caused by inaccurate reading

☐ Make appear small by comparison

☐ One of the tendons at the back of the knee

☐ Acquire or deserve by one's efforts or actions

☐ Covered with beads of liquid

☐ Tiny particle of protoplasm found in vertebrate blood; essential for blood clotting

Week #______ From _____/_____/_____ to _____/_____/_____

Date	Weekday	Morning	Afternoon	Evening
	Monday			
	Tuesday			
	Wednesday			
	Thursday			
	Friday			
	Saturday			
	Sunday			

Notes

1 converted	6 acquiesce	11 discredit
2 rheumatoid	7 disapprove	12 richness
3 staunch	8 repressed	13 deprivation
4 formative	9 torpedo	14 managerial
5 assigned	10 enchantment	15 unreal

☐ Minimal language unit that has a syntactic function

☐ Firm and dependable especially in loyalty

☐ To agree or express agreement

☐ Characterized by or showing the suppression of impulses or emotions

☐ A state of extreme poverty

☐ Consider bad or wrong

☐ Lacking in reality or substance or genuineness; not corresponding to acknowledged facts or criteria

☐ A feeling of great liking for something wonderful and unusual

☐ Appointed to a post or duty

☐ The state of being held in low esteem

☐ Spiritually reborn or having changed religion

☐ Of or pertaining to arthritis

☐ A professional killer who uses a gun

☐ Of or relating to the function or responsibility or activity of management

☐ The property of being extremely abundant

Week #_______ From ____/____/____ to ____/____/____

Date	Weekday	Morning	Afternoon	Evening
	Monday			
	Tuesday			
	Wednesday			
	Thursday			
	Friday			
	Saturday			
	Sunday			

Notes

1 martyrdom	6 contracted	11 panoramic
2 oxymoron	7 aural	12 bully
3 cramp	8 petitioner	13 celestial
4 chemist	9 skunk	14 outlandish
5 plating	10 password	15 proffer

- [ ] A secret word or phrase known only to a restricted group
- [ ] Conjoining contradictory terms
- [ ] A scientist who specializes in chemistry
- [ ] Reduced in size or pulled together
- [ ] As from an altitude or distance
- [ ] Present for acceptance or rejection
- [ ] Conspicuously or grossly unconventional or unusual
- [ ] Of or pertaining to hearing or the ear
- [ ] Of or relating to the sky
- [ ] One praying humbly for something
- [ ] A person who is deemed to be despicable or contemptible
- [ ] An uncultured, aggressive, rude, noisy troublemaker
- [ ] Death that is imposed because of the person's adherence of a religious faith or cause
- [ ] A thin coating of metal deposited on a surface
- [ ] A painful and involuntary muscular contraction

Week #_____ From ____/____/____ to ____/____/____

Date	Weekday	Morning	Afternoon	Evening
	Monday			
	Tuesday			
	Wednesday			
	Thursday			
	Friday			
	Saturday			
	Sunday			

Notes

1 heyday	6 majestic	11 siding
2 invading	7 sandstone	12 promoter
3 forerunner	8 sensational	13 dredge
4 distress	9 manipulator	14 credence
5 poisonous	10 propane	15 appendix

☐ Superior to mundane matters, having a god-like quality

☐ Psychological suffering

☐ A sedimentary rock consisting of sand consolidated with some cement

☐ A person who goes before or announces the coming of another

☐ The mental attitude that something is believable and should be accepted as true

☐ Someone who is an active supporter and advocate

☐ A short stretch of railway track used to store rolling stock or enable trains on the same line to pass

☐ An agent that operates some apparatus or machine

☐ A power shovel to remove material from a channel or riverbed

☐ The period of greatest prosperity or productivity

☐ Supplementary material that is collected and appended at the back of a book, article or document

☐ Involving invasion or aggressive attack

☐ Causing intense interest, curiosity, or emotion

☐ Colorless gas found in natural gas and petroleum; used as a fuel

☐ Having the qualities or effects of a poison

Week #_______ From _____/_____/_____ to _____/_____/_____

Date	Weekday	Morning	Afternoon	Evening
	Monday			
	Tuesday			
	Wednesday			
	Thursday			
	Friday			
	Saturday			
	Sunday			

Notes

1 neuroscientist	6 juggernaut	11 precedence
2 brutality	7 content	12 ignition
3 away	8 subsidized	13 documented
4 codify	9 calamity	14 moth
5 disconcerting	10 expound	15 yoke

- [ ] Typically crepuscular or nocturnal insect having a stout body and feathery or hairlike antennae

- [ ] Status established in order of importance or urgency

- [ ] Add details, as to an account or idea; clarify the meaning of and discourse in a learned way, usually in writing

- [ ] An event resulting in great loss and misfortune

- [ ] Having partial financial support from public funds

- [ ] The trait of extreme cruelty

- [ ] A massive inexorable force that seems to crush everything in its way

- [ ] Everything that is included in a collection and that is held or included in something

- [ ] From a particular thing, place or position

- [ ] Furnished with or supported by documents

- [ ] The process of initiating combustion or catching fire

- [ ] Fabric comprising a fitted part at the top of a garment

- [ ] Organize into a code or system, such as a body of law

- [ ] A neurobiologist who specializes in the study of the brain

- [ ] Causing an emotional disturbance

Week #______ From ____/____/____ to ____/____/____

Date	Weekday	Morning	Afternoon	Evening
	Monday			
	Tuesday			
	Wednesday			
	Thursday			
	Friday			
	Saturday			
	Sunday			

Notes

1	subdue	6	ingenuity	11	sigma
2	realignment	7	quiz	12	tabernacle
3	defense	8	uncooperative	13	furor
4	hoard	9	loudness	14	sweating
5	secede	10	serotonin	15	clam

☐ Unwilling to cooperate

☐ The magnitude of sound

☐ Put down by force or intimidation

☐ Withdraw from an organization or communion

☐ The process of the sweat glands of the skin secreting a salty fluid

☐ An examination consisting of a few short questions

☐ A neurotransmitter involved in sleep, depression and memory

☐ An interest followed with exaggerated zeal

☐ The 18th letter of the Greek alphabet

☐ The place of worship for a Jewish congregation

☐ A secret store of valuables or money

☐ The power of creative imagination

☐ Burrowing marine mollusk living on sand or mud; the shell closes with viselike firmness

☐ The act of adjusting again

☐ Military action or resources protecting a country against potential enemies

Week #_____ From ____/____/____ to ____/____/____

Date	Weekday	Morning	Afternoon	Evening
	Monday			
	Tuesday			
	Wednesday			
	Thursday			
	Friday			
	Saturday			
	Sunday			

Notes

1	overt	6	rash	11	shrinkage
2	exhilarating	7	sojourner	12	coupon
3	intoxicate	8	regularity	13	invasive
4	trepidation	9	eulogy	14	peculiarity
5	impartial	10	must	15	artful

- [ ] A negotiable certificate that can be detached and redeemed as needed
- [ ] Imprudently incurring risk
- [ ] A temporary resident
- [ ] Process or result of becoming less or smaller
- [ ] Making lively and cheerful
- [ ] Not straightforward or candid; giving a false appearance of frankness
- [ ] Be compelled, be necessary, have to, ought to
- [ ] A formal expression of praise for someone who has died recently
- [ ] A feeling of alarm or dread
- [ ] Showing lack of favoritism
- [ ] Observable; not secret or hidden
- [ ] Fill with high spirits; fill with optimism
- [ ] A property of polygons: the property of having equal sides and equal angles
- [ ] Relating to a technique in which the body is entered by puncture or incision
- [ ] An odd or unusual characteristic

Week #_______ From ______/______/______ to ______/______/______

Date	Weekday	Morning	Afternoon	Evening
	Monday			
	Tuesday			
	Wednesday			
	Thursday			
	Friday			
	Saturday			
	Sunday			

Notes

1	citrus	6	glucose	11	lowering
2	ambivalence	7	reiterate	12	steppe
3	fundamentalism	8	synapse	13	ancillary
4	bran	9	dissenting	14	optic
5	angular	10	standardize	15	insightful

☐ Broken husks of the seeds of cereal grains that are separated from the flour by sifting

☐ The junction between two neurons or between a neuron and a muscle

☐ Measured by an angle or by the rate of change of an angle

☐ Furnishing added support

☐ Disagreeing, especially with a majority

☐ The act of causing to become less

☐ The interpretation of every word in the sacred texts as literal truth

☐ Cause to conform to standard or norm

☐ Of or relating to or resembling the eye

☐ A monosaccharide sugar that has several forms; an important source of physiological energy

☐ To say, state, or perform again

☐ Mixed feelings or emotions

☐ Exhibiting insight or clear and deep perception

☐ Any of numerous fruits of the genus Citrus having thick rind and juicy pulp; grown in warm regions

☐ Extensive plain without trees

Week #______ From ____/____/____   to ____/____/____

Date	Weekday	Morning	Afternoon	Evening
	Monday			
	Tuesday			
	Wednesday			
	Thursday			
	Friday			
	Saturday			
	Sunday			

Notes

➤
➤
➤
➤
➤
➤
➤
➤
➤
➤
➤
➤
➤
➤
➤
➤
➤
➤

1	schoolchild	6	glean	11	discount
2	ethereal	7	housewife	12	landed
3	sincerity	8	supercomputer	13	ferocious
4	symptomatic	9	dogmatism	14	broker
5	rekindle	10	amputee	15	riddle

- [ ] Gather, as of natural products

- [ ] A reduction in the selling price of something

- [ ] Someone who has had a limb removed by amputation

- [ ] Characteristic or indicative of a disease

- [ ] A wife who manages a household while her husband earns the family income

- [ ] Owning or consisting of land or real estate

- [ ] Pierce with many holes

- [ ] Kindle anew, as of a fire

- [ ] A businessman who buys or sells for another in exchange for a commission

- [ ] A young person attending school

- [ ] Characterized by lightness and insubstantiality; as impalpable or intangible as air

- [ ] An earnest and sincere feeling

- [ ] A mainframe computer that is one of the most powerful available at a given time

- [ ] The intolerance and prejudice of a bigot

- [ ] Marked by extreme and violent energy

Week #_______ From _____/_____/_____   to _____/_____/_____

Date	Weekday	Morning	Afternoon	Evening
	Monday			
	Tuesday			
	Wednesday			
	Thursday			
	Friday			
	Saturday			
	Sunday			

Notes

Quiz **81**

1 ambient	6 contemporaneous	11 commandment
2 misgiving	7 sulfuric	12 unconcerned
3 inspirational	8 longitude	13 electromagnetic
4 minuscule	9 affront	14 philanthropy
5 diviner	10 equestrian	15 resolute

☐ Uneasiness about the fitness of an action

☐ Completely enveloping

☐ Of or relating to or composed of knights

☐ Someone who claims to discover hidden knowledge with the aid of supernatural powers

☐ Firm in purpose or belief; characterized by firmness and determination

☐ Of or relating to a small cursive script developed from uncial; 7th to 9th centuries

☐ A deliberately offensive act or something producing the effect of deliberate disrespect

☐ Occurring in the same period of time

☐ Voluntary promotion of human welfare

☐ Lacking in interest, care or feeling

☐ Imparting a divine influence on the mind and soul

☐ The angular distance between a point on any meridian and the prime meridian at Greenwich

☐ Of or relating to or containing sulfur

☐ Pertaining to or exhibiting magnetism produced by electric charge in motion

☐ Something that is commanded

Week #_____ From ___/___/___ to ___/___/___

Date	Weekday	Morning	Afternoon	Evening
	Monday			
	Tuesday			
	Wednesday			
	Thursday			
	Friday			
	Saturday			
	Sunday			

Notes

1	mystique	6	exalt	11	monastic
2	derision	7	resurgence	12	captive
3	radioactivity	8	savagery	13	vigil
4	suppression	9	farce	14	cosmopolitan
5	restorative	10	thickness	15	unspoken

- [ ] A person who is confined; especially a prisoner of war
- [ ] The dimension through an object as opposed to its length or width
- [ ] Praise, glorify, or honor
- [ ] Tending to impart new life and vigor to
- [ ] A period of sleeplessness
- [ ] An aura of heightened value or interest or meaning surrounding a person or thing
- [ ] Of communal life sequestered from the world under religious vows
- [ ] Growing or occurring in many parts of the world
- [ ] The property of being untamed and ferocious
- [ ] Bringing again into activity and prominence
- [ ] Expressed without speech
- [ ] A comedy characterized by broad satire and improbable situations
- [ ] Forceful prevention; putting down by power or authority
- [ ] Contemptuous laughter
- [ ] The spontaneous emission of a stream of particles or electromagnetic rays in nuclear decay

Week #_______ From ______/______/______ to ______/______/______

Date	Weekday	Morning	Afternoon	Evening
	Monday			
	Tuesday			
	Wednesday			
	Thursday			
	Friday			
	Saturday			
	Sunday			

Notes

1	shellfish	6	remediation	11	objectionable
2	trappings	7	hospitalization	12	spate
3	striving	8	patronizing	13	downplay
4	edifice	9	audacious	14	unconnected
5	dizziness	10	waste	15	disarray

☐ Act of correcting an error or a fault or an evil

☐ An effortful attempt to attain a goal

☐ A structure that has a roof and walls and stands more or less permanently in one place

☐ Spend thoughtlessly; throw away

☐ Accessory wearing apparel

☐ Not joined or linked together

☐ A reeling sensation; a feeling that you are about to fall

☐ A period of time when you are confined to a hospital

☐ Meat of edible aquatic invertebrate with a shell

☐ Characteristic of those who treat others with condescension

☐ Causing disapproval or protest

☐ Represent as less significant or important

☐ Invulnerable to fear or intimidation

☐ A mental state characterized by a lack of clear and orderly thought and behavior

☐ A large number, amount or extent

Week #_______ From ____/____/____ to ____/____/____

Date	Weekday	Morning	Afternoon	Evening
	Monday			
	Tuesday			
	Wednesday			
	Thursday			
	Friday			
	Saturday			
	Sunday			

Notes

>

>

>

>

>

>

>

>

>

>

>

>

>

>

>

>

>

Quiz **84**

1 etching	6 marshal	11 alchemy
2 widget	7 wafer	12 classified
3 shameful	8 counterbalance	13 anaerobic
4 complacent	9 metaphysics	14 internally
5 hasten	10 clover	15 wondrous

- [ ] Act or move at high speed
- [ ] Something unspecified whose name is either forgotten or not known
- [ ] A law officer having duties similar to those of a sheriff in carrying out the judgments of a court of law
- [ ] Uncritically satisfied with oneself or one's actions; not looking to improve
- [ ] A small adhesive disk of paste; used to seal letters
- [ ] On or from the inside
- [ ] A plant of the genus Trifolium
- [ ] An impression made from an etched plate
- [ ] The philosophical study of being and knowing
- [ ] Living or active in the absence of free oxygen
- [ ] The way two individuals relate to each other
- [ ] Extraordinarily good or great; used especially as an intensifier
- [ ] Deserving or bringing disgrace or shame
- [ ] Arranged into classes
- [ ] A weight that balances another weight

Week #_____ From ____/____/____ to ____/____/____

Date	Weekday	Morning	Afternoon	Evening
	Monday			
	Tuesday			
	Wednesday			
	Thursday			
	Friday			
	Saturday			
	Sunday			

Notes

1	ambulatory	6	anvil	11	consequential
2	forgo	7	trusting	12	skyscraper
3	transmitted	8	distinguishable	13	conscientious
4	ombudsman	9	crucifix	14	taxation
5	herbivore	10	condone	15	ruse

- [ ] A very tall building with many stories
- [ ] Having important issues or results
- [ ] Charge against a citizen's person, property or activity for the support of government
- [ ] Do without or cease to hold or adhere to
- [ ] Relating to or adapted for walking
- [ ] Any animal that feeds chiefly on grass and other plants
- [ ] A government appointee who investigates complaints by private persons against the government
- [ ] Characterized by extreme care and great effort
- [ ] Representation of the cross on which Jesus died
- [ ] Inclined to believe or confide readily; full of trust
- [ ] Capable of being perceived as different or distinct
- [ ] A deceptive maneuver
- [ ] Excuse, overlook, or make allowances for; be lenient with
- [ ] Occurring among members of a family usually by heredity
- [ ] A heavy block of iron or steel on which hot metals are shaped by hammering

Week #_______ From _____/_____/_____ to _____/_____/_____

Date	Weekday	Morning	Afternoon	Evening
	Monday			
	Tuesday			
	Wednesday			
	Thursday			
	Friday			
	Saturday			
	Sunday			

Notes

1 gastric	6 mackerel	11 alertness
2 rapport	7 dramatist	12 confederacy
3 adverb	8 beggar	13 dowry
4 pathology	9 watcher	14 jurisprudence
5 nausea	10 magnate	15 gripping

☐ Money or property brought by a woman to her husband at marriage

☐ A very wealthy or powerful businessman

☐ Someone who writes plays

☐ A relationship of mutual understanding or trust and agreement between people

☐ A union of political organizations

☐ A pauper who lives by begging

☐ Flesh of very important usually small fatty Atlantic fish

☐ Relating to or involving the stomach

☐ A close observer; someone who looks at something

☐ The state that precedes vomiting

☐ The branch of medical science that studies the causes and nature and effects of diseases

☐ The word class that qualifies verbs or clauses

☐ The process of paying close and continuous attention

☐ The branch of philosophy concerned with the law and the principles that lead courts to make the decisions they do

☐ Capable of arousing and holding the attention

Week #______ From ____/____/____   to ____/____/____

Date	Weekday	Morning	Afternoon	Evening
	Monday			
	Tuesday			
	Wednesday			
	Thursday			
	Friday			
	Saturday			
	Sunday			

Notes

1 windrow	6 conflagration	11 foreshadow
2 amorphous	7 perceptible	12 corona
3 disjointed	8 iconoclastic	13 zoology
4 mechanization	9 eradication	14 feat
5 voracious	10 exclamation	15 eclipse

☐ A very intense and uncontrolled fire

☐ Having no definite form or distinct shape

☐ The condition of having a highly technical implementation

☐ Be a sign of something to come, especially something important or bad

☐ Lacking orderly continuity

☐ Excessively greedy and grasping

☐ An abrupt excited utterance

☐ Characterized by attack on established beliefs or institutions

☐ All the animal life in a particular region or period

☐ Capable of being perceived by the mind or senses

☐ The complete destruction of every trace of something

☐ The blocking or partial blocking of light from one celestial body by another celestial body

☐ The outermost region of the sun's atmosphere; visible as a white halo during a solar eclipse

☐ A notable achievement

☐ A row or line of hay raked together for the purpose of being rolled into cocks or heaps

Week #_______ From _____/_____/_____ to _____/_____/_____

Date	Weekday	Morning	Afternoon	Evening
	Monday			
	Tuesday			
	Wednesday			
	Thursday			
	Friday			
	Saturday			
	Sunday			

Notes

1 logger	6 jeopardy	11 favored
2 remedial	7 sheath	12 goad
3 quad	8 phantom	13 swath
4 anemia	9 modulate	14 bereavement
5 sloping	10 airspace	15 shading

☐ Give heart or courage to

☐ The space in the atmosphere immediately above the earth

☐ A source of danger; a possibility of incurring loss or misfortune

☐ State of sorrow over the death or departure of a loved one

☐ A protective covering

☐ One of four children born at the same time from the same pregnancy

☐ Valued more than all others, often treated with partiality

☐ Having an oblique or slanted direction

☐ A person who fells trees

☐ Change the key of, in music

☐ A deficiency of red blood cells

☐ A broad area or strip of something

☐ A ghostly appearing figure

☐ Tending or intended to rectify or improve

☐ Graded markings that indicate light or shaded areas in a drawing or painting

Week #_______ From ____/____/____ to ____/____/____

Date	Weekday	Morning	Afternoon	Evening
	Monday			
	Tuesday			
	Wednesday			
	Thursday			
	Friday			
	Saturday			
	Sunday			

Notes

1 word	6 detachment	11 envelop
2 bile	7 pictorial	12 superhuman
3 volley	8 meditate	13 sporadic
4 anomaly	9 guidebook	14 prompting
5 gatekeeper	10 oftentimes	15 soybean

☐ Rapid simultaneous discharge of firearms

☐ A unit of language that native speakers can identify

☐ Avoiding emotional involvement

☐ Above or beyond the human or demanding more than human power or endurance

☐ A digestive juice secreted by the liver and stored in the gallbladder; aids in the digestion of fats

☐ Someone who controls access to something

☐ Think deeply about a subject or question over a period of time

☐ Recurring in scattered and irregular or unpredictable instances

☐ Many times at short intervals

☐ Something that offers basic information or instruction

☐ Persuasion formulated as a suggestion

☐ Deviation from the normal or common order or form or rule

☐ Enclose or enfold completely with or as if with a covering

☐ A source of oil; used for forage and soil improvement and as food

☐ Pertaining to or consisting of pictures

Week #______ From ____/____/____ to ____/____/____

Date	Weekday	Morning	Afternoon	Evening
	Monday			
	Tuesday			
	Wednesday			
	Thursday			
	Friday			
	Saturday			
	Sunday			

Notes

1	scarcity	6	plural	11	retool
2	eloquent	7	asthmatic	12	judgement
3	acoustic	8	accolade	13	rigidity
4	facsimile	9	discerning	14	morph
5	connoisseur	10	robotic	15	irreducible

☐ Relating to breathing with a whistling sound

☐ Having or revealing keen insight and good judgment

☐ An exact copy or reproduction

☐ The legal document stating the reasons for a judicial decision

☐ Reorganize, especially for the purpose of updating and improving

☐ A small and inadequate amount

☐ Of or relating to the science of acoustics

☐ Of or relating to mechanical robots

☐ Speaking readily, clearly, and effectively

☐ Incapable of being made smaller or simpler

☐ Composed of more than one member, set, or kind

☐ The physical property of being stiff and resisting bending

☐ A tangible symbol signifying approval or distinction

☐ An expert able to appreciate a field; especially in the fine arts

☐ Cause to change shape in a computer animation

Week #_____ From ____/____/____ to ____/____/____

Date	Weekday	Morning	Afternoon	Evening
	Monday			
	Tuesday			
	Wednesday			
	Thursday			
	Friday			
	Saturday			
	Sunday			

Notes

1	token	6	royalist	11	mishap
2	tanker	7	populist	12	video
3	idealist	8	premarital	13	pointedly
4	monotheism	9	shoulder	14	temp
5	zoom	10	submerge	15	junta

- [ ] Relating to events before a marriage
- [ ] Something serving as a sign of something else
- [ ] The visible part of a television transmission
- [ ] Move along very quickly
- [ ] An unpredictable outcome that is unfortunate
- [ ] A worker hired on a temporary basis
- [ ] An advocate of democratic principles
- [ ] Belief in a single God
- [ ] An advocate of the principles of monarchy
- [ ] In such a manner as to make something clearly evident
- [ ] Someone guided more by ideals than by practical considerations
- [ ] The part of the body between the neck and the upper arm
- [ ] A cargo ship designed to carry crude oil in bulk
- [ ] Sink below the surface; go under or as if under water
- [ ] A group of military officers who rule a country after seizing power

Week #______ From _____/_____/_____ to _____/_____/_____

Date	Weekday	Morning	Afternoon	Evening
	Monday			
	Tuesday			
	Wednesday			
	Thursday			
	Friday			
	Saturday			
	Sunday			

Notes

1	heroism	6	retaliatory	11	permanence
2	morbid	7	statehood	12	brig
3	narcissism	8	quantifiable	13	municipality
4	unsubstantiated	9	stray	14	indefinite
5	craftsmanship	10	incendiary	15	respite

☐ An exceptional interest in and admiration for yourself

☐ Suggesting an unhealthy mental state

☐ Of or relating to or having the nature of retribution

☐ A relief from harm or discomfort

☐ Skill in an occupation or trade

☐ An urban district having corporate status and powers of self-government

☐ Vague or not clearly defined or stated

☐ Involving deliberate burning of property

☐ Move about aimlessly or without any destination, often in search of food or employment

☐ Two-masted sailing vessel square-rigged on both masts

☐ The qualities of a hero or heroine; exceptional or heroic courage when facing danger

☐ Capable of being quantified

☐ The property of being able to exist for an indefinite duration

☐ The condition of being a state

☐ Unsupported by other evidence

Week #_______ From _____/_____/_____ to _____/_____/_____

Date	Weekday	Morning	Afternoon	Evening
	Monday			
	Tuesday			
	Wednesday			
	Thursday			
	Friday			
	Saturday			
	Sunday			

Notes

Q u i z **93**

1	moor	6	fallout	11	reorganization
2	inconsequential	7	supposition	12	diligence
3	sarcoma	8	schematic	13	songbird
4	needless	9	receptacle	14	changeable
5	appall	10	principality	15	sensuous

☐ Open land usually with peaty soil covered with heather and bracken and moss

☐ Conscientiousness in paying proper attention to a task; giving the degree of care required in a given situation

☐ Lacking worth or importance

☐ A message expressing an opinion based on incomplete evidence

☐ Represented in simplified or symbolic form

☐ Strike with disgust or revulsion

☐ Taking delight in beauty

☐ The radioactive particles that settle to the ground after a nuclear explosion

☐ Territory ruled by a prince

☐ Any bird having a musical call

☐ A usually malignant tumor arising from connective tissue; one of the four major types of cancer

☐ Capable of or tending to change in form or quality or nature

☐ A container that is used to put or keep things in

☐ The imposition of a new organization; organizing differently

☐ Unnecessary and unwarranted

Week #_____ From ____/____/____ to ____/____/____

Date	Weekday	Morning	Afternoon	Evening
	Monday			
	Tuesday			
	Wednesday			
	Thursday			
	Friday			
	Saturday			
	Sunday			

Notes

1	skew	6	pathogenic	11	interlocking
2	delineate	7	retribution	12	smog
3	temperate	8	meld	13	pretext
4	nakedness	9	servicing	14	innate
5	purify	10	unsophisticated	15	theta

- [ ] Remove impurities from, increase the concentration of, and separate through the process of distillation

- [ ] Not wise in the ways of the world

- [ ] Something serving to conceal plans; a fictitious reason that is concocted in order to conceal the real reason

- [ ] Announce for a score; of cards in a card game

- [ ] The state of being without clothing or covering of any kind

- [ ] Represented accurately or precisely

- [ ] Linked or locked closely together as by dovetailing

- [ ] The 8th letter of the Greek alphabet

- [ ] Not established by conditioning or learning

- [ ] Free from extremes; mild; or characteristic of such weather or climate

- [ ] A justly deserved penalty

- [ ] Having an oblique or slanting direction or position

- [ ] The act of mating by male animals

- [ ] Able to cause disease

- [ ] Air pollution by a mixture of smoke and fog

Week #_______ From ____/____/____ to ____/____/____

Date	Weekday	Morning	Afternoon	Evening
	Monday			
	Tuesday			
	Wednesday			
	Thursday			
	Friday			
	Saturday			
	Sunday			

Notes

1 edited	6 counterpoint	11 pointer
2 proximate	7 inordinate	12 neurologist
3 exacting	8 exemplar	13 reassess
4 nourish	9 courier	14 side
5 patriarchy	10 erstwhile	15 provisional

☐ Improved or corrected by critical editing

☐ A person who carries a message

☐ Something to be imitated

☐ Under terms not final or fully worked out or agreed upon

☐ Beyond normal limits

☐ A form of social organization in which a male is the family head and title is traced through the male line

☐ A place within a region identified relative to a center or reference location

☐ Belonging to some prior time

☐ Severe and unremitting in making demands

☐ A mark to indicate a direction or relation

☐ Revise or renew one's assessment

☐ A medical specialist in the nervous system and the disorders affecting it

☐ A musical form involving the simultaneous sound of two or more melodies

☐ Provide with nourishment

☐ Closest in degree or order especially in a chain of causes and effects

Week #_____ From ____/____/____ to ____/____/____

Date	Weekday	Morning	Afternoon	Evening
	Monday			
	Tuesday			
	Wednesday			
	Thursday			
	Friday			
	Saturday			
	Sunday			

Notes

1	isolationism	6	perceptive	11	idealized
2	slippage	7	gorge	12	furnace
3	pollute	8	formaldehyde	13	evocation
4	tantalize	9	cycle	14	progressively
5	infestation	10	hallucination	15	reforestation

- [ ] A colorless poisonous gas; made by the oxidation of methanol

- [ ] Exalted to an ideal perfection or excellence

- [ ] Illusory perception; a common symptom of severe mental disorder

- [ ] An interval during which a recurring sequence of events occurs

- [ ] Advancing in amount or intensity

- [ ] Excite or tease by presenting or offering something desirable, especially when it is unobtainable

- [ ] An enclosed chamber in which heat is produced to heat buildings, destroy refuse, smelt or refine ores, etc

- [ ] Overeat or eat immodestly; make a pig of oneself

- [ ] The restoration of a forest that had been reduced by fire or cutting

- [ ] The state of being invaded or overrun by parasites

- [ ] Of or relating to perception

- [ ] A decrease of transmitted power in a mechanical system caused by slipping

- [ ] Make impure in a bad way; make something harmful, especially by the addition of some unwanted substance

- [ ] A policy of nonparticipation in international economic and political relations

- [ ] Imaginative re-creation

Week #_______ From _____/_____/_____ to _____/_____/_____

Date	Weekday	Morning	Afternoon	Evening
	Monday			
	Tuesday			
	Wednesday			
	Thursday			
	Friday			
	Saturday			
	Sunday			

Notes

1	merciful	6	unnatural	11	innocuous
2	obscene	7	diminishing	12	empress
3	anchorage	8	zombie	13	unhappiness
4	totalitarian	9	tutelage	14	resettle
5	sanctity	10	sanguine	15	intricacy

The quality of being holy

Marked by elaborately complex detail

Designed to incite to indecency or lust

Confidently optimistic and cheerful

A woman emperor or the wife of an emperor

Not in accordance with or determined by nature; contrary to nature

A dead body that has been brought back to life by a supernatural force

The training or instruction provided by a teacher or tutor

Settle in a new place

Becoming smaller, less or appearing to do so

Not injurious to physical or mental health

Showing or giving mercy

Emotions experienced when not in a state of well-being

The condition of being secured to a base

Characterized by a government in which the political authority exercises absolute and centralized control

Week #_____ From ___/___/___ to ___/___/___

Date	Weekday	Morning	Afternoon	Evening
	Monday			
	Tuesday			
	Wednesday			
	Thursday			
	Friday			
	Saturday			
	Sunday			

Notes

1 deft	6 annuity	11 foreboding
2 ramification	7 tonsil	12 manliness
3 churchman	8 nocturnal	13 born
4 major	9 employed	14 mortuary
5 crusader	10 magenta	15 accredit

- [ ] Of or relating to or characteristic of death

- [ ] Of deep purplish red

- [ ] A feeling of evil to come

- [ ] A clergyman or other person in religious orders

- [ ] Either of two masses of lymphatic tissue one on each side of the oral pharynx

- [ ] Brought into existence

- [ ] A disputant who advocates reform

- [ ] Grant credentials to

- [ ] Of greater importance, stature or rank

- [ ] Having your services engaged for; or having a job especially one that pays wages or a salary

- [ ] The act of branching out or dividing into branches

- [ ] Belonging to or active during the night

- [ ] The trait of being manly; having the characteristics of an adult male

- [ ] Income from capital investment paid in a series of regular payments

- [ ] Skillful in physical movements; especially of the hands

Week #_____ From ___/___/___ to ___/___/___

Date	Weekday	Morning	Afternoon	Evening
	Monday			
	Tuesday			
	Wednesday			
	Thursday			
	Friday			
	Saturday			
	Sunday			

Notes

1 terrifying	6 headscarf	11 decode
2 measurable	7 clipping	12 size
3 microprocessor	8 contagious	13 combative
4 tame	9 namesake	14 manufacture
5 loath	10 distorted	15 cherish

- So badly formed or out of shape as to be ugly

- Capable of being measured

- Put together out of artificial or natural components or parts

- Integrated circuit semiconductor chip that performs the bulk of the processing and controls the parts of a system

- Easily diffused or spread as from one person to another

- Be fond of; be attached to

- An excerpt cut from a newspaper or magazine

- Convert code into ordinary language

- A kerchief worn over the head and tied under the chin

- Unwillingness to do something contrary to your custom

- Inclined or showing an inclination to dispute or disagree, even to engage in law suits

- Correct by punishment or discipline

- The physical magnitude of something

- A person with the same name as another

- Causing extreme terror

Week #_______ From ____/____/____ to ____/____/____

Date	Weekday	Morning	Afternoon	Evening
	Monday			
	Tuesday			
	Wednesday			
	Thursday			
	Friday			
	Saturday			
	Sunday			

Notes

1	paramount	6	whiteness	11	intercession
2	volatility	7	contemplation	12	implement
3	anatomical	8	dilute	13	anomalous
4	liberated	9	modernism	14	dialog
5	piping	10	nomenclature	15	emulate

☐ A thin strip of covered cord used to edge hems

☐ Released from chemical combination

☐ Strive to equal or match, especially by imitating

☐ A conversation between two persons

☐ Of or relating to the structure of the body

☐ The quality or state of the achromatic color of greatest lightness

☐ Lessen the strength or flavor of a solution or mixture

☐ A prayer to God on behalf of another person

☐ A long and thoughtful observation

☐ A system of words used to name things in a particular discipline

☐ Apply in a manner consistent with its purpose or design

☐ Genre of art and literature that makes a self-conscious break with previous genres

☐ The property of changing readily from a solid or liquid to a vapor

☐ Having superior power and influence

☐ Deviating from the general or common order or type

Week #_______ From _____/_____/_____ to _____/_____/_____

Date	Weekday	Morning	Afternoon	Evening
	Monday			
	Tuesday			
	Wednesday			
	Thursday			
	Friday			
	Saturday			
	Sunday			

Notes

➢
➢
➢
➢
➢
➢
➢
➢
➢
➢
➢
➢
➢
➢
➢
➢
➢
➢
➢

2
Answers

<u>2. ANSWERS</u>

Q1	Q2	Q3	Q4	Q5	Q6	Q7	Q8	Q9	Q10
2	6	11	7	4	1	2	11	4	14
3	13	6	13	1	7	8	14	15	2
10	7	2	2	8	3	1	8	3	5
11	15	13	10	14	2	9	2	13	13
15	14	10	1	3	9	3	12	12	3
6	12	1	11	15	11	6	1	11	1
9	5	3	12	11	4	13	3	7	7
1	3	5	8	10	14	15	6	9	10
8	4	4	6	2	6	10	13	2	4
4	2	12	4	5	15	5	9	1	11
5	11	7	14	7	10	12	7	14	6
14	10	9	9	6	8	14	10	10	8
13	1	8	3	13	12	7	15	6	15
12	9	15	15	9	5	4	5	8	12
7	8	14	5	12	13	11	4	5	9

Q11	Q12	Q13	Q14	Q15	Q16	Q17	Q18	Q19	Q20
1	4	6	13	3	6	7	9	8	5
6	1	9	15	12	4	3	7	1	10
8	6	4	5	7	14	6	12	12	13
5	12	5	11	11	15	12	4	10	8
3	2	12	8	10	8	14	5	15	14
9	7	1	7	13	7	10	2	5	15
2	5	11	3	1	11	13	15	14	1
7	10	13	9	2	10	2	14	4	3
15	14	8	2	9	13	15	8	13	2
12	3	15	12	5	2	11	1	3	4
10	8	7	4	14	12	8	10	11	12
11	15	3	6	4	9	5	6	6	7
13	9	10	14	8	5	1	13	2	6
14	13	2	1	15	3	4	3	7	11
4	11	14	10	6	1	9	11	9	9

<u>2. ANSWERS</u>

Q21	Q22	Q23	Q24	Q25	Q26	Q27	Q28	Q29	Q30
13	9	5	14	12	12	4	9	11	7
11	15	6	5	9	3	13	5	1	6
9	7	11	10	8	2	14	8	2	2
10	8	2	3	14	15	10	2	9	4
3	11	9	6	2	9	2	15	7	14
15	3	7	8	13	5	6	7	15	5
6	14	1	9	6	7	11	10	6	10
7	6	4	13	1	14	8	13	5	8
8	12	12	15	5	11	3	4	13	9
12	13	8	7	4	13	1	12	4	11
5	4	13	1	3	10	15	11	10	3
2	5	10	2	10	8	7	6	3	13
4	2	14	4	7	6	12	1	8	15
1	1	15	11	15	4	5	14	12	12
13	10	3	12	11	1	9	3	14	1

Q31	Q32	Q33	Q34	Q35	Q36	Q37	Q38	Q39	Q40
7	4	11	6	3	12	9	13	10	15
12	9	2	13	15	2	2	8	11	8
6	11	13	3	2	15	3	11	4	4
14	14	14	4	4	7	10	5	7	12
3	13	10	14	8	11	1	3	14	5
15	15	4	8	5	3	7	9	15	13
2	2	15	15	1	5	5	1	8	7
4	1	9	7	11	6	13	6	2	14
11	12	6	1	12	4	8	15	1	1
13	7	7	2	14	10	12	10	3	2
8	5	8	5	13	8	4	2	5	6
10	10	5	9	9	9	15	4	9	11
1	3	3	10	10	1	14	12	12	10
9	6	1	12	7	14	11	7	6	3
5	8	12	11	6	13	6	14	13	9

<u>2. ANSWERS</u>

Q41	Q42	Q43	Q44	Q45	Q46	Q47	Q48	Q49	Q50
5	8	9	8	2	2	14	4	2	12
14	9	2	14	8	7	1	15	3	7
10	10	11	6	9	13	6	5	12	14
6	13	14	3	11	15	10	13	4	15
8	12	12	7	3	11	11	3	5	13
2	3	4	2	13	8	12	12	11	4
13	6	8	11	10	9	15	8	1	8
4	5	10	13	6	5	9	1	7	6
9	7	6	1	12	1	7	2	14	11
7	4	15	12	14	10	2	10	6	9
12	1	3	4	1	4	3	11	15	10
11	11	7	5	7	6	5	9	8	5
1	15	1	9	5	12	13	14	9	3
3	14	13	10	4	14	4	6	10	2
15	2	5	15	15	3	8	7	13	1

Q51	Q52	Q53	Q54	Q55	Q56	Q57	Q58	Q59	Q60
10	1	13	15	6	14	12	6	9	8
5	5	11	1	1	2	5	11	7	4
2	8	12	11	5	10	2	8	2	15
14	3	6	6	12	7	14	12	3	5
4	4	7	10	8	8	8	14	14	13
11	13	4	2	9	4	10	4	4	12
12	2	8	5	13	6	9	10	10	3
13	15	2	14	14	11	6	7	5	9
7	6	10	8	11	9	7	13	11	14
8	9	5	9	2	5	3	15	15	11
3	7	14	7	7	13	15	3	6	7
9	14	1	12	10	12	11	2	8	1
1	11	3	4	15	15	4	5	1	10
15	10	15	3	3	3	13	1	12	2
6	12	9	13	4	1	1	9	13	6

<u>2. ANSWERS</u>

Q61	Q62	Q63	Q64	Q65	Q66	Q67	Q68	Q69	Q70
2	12	3	10	7	8	4	9	8	2
9	14	5	4	6	2	9	11	6	14
10	13	8	14	1	1	15	15	12	11
15	4	2	2	2	5	8	12	1	15
11	6	11	5	4	14	1	5	3	13
14	8	12	15	13	4	6	2	5	7
8	5	15	1	9	9	2	10	7	1
3	15	10	13	12	12	14	8	11	10
12	10	6	6	14	15	11	4	14	12
6	11	13	11	15	10	10	14	13	4
4	9	14	12	3	6	13	13	15	3
13	1	7	7	10	7	3	1	10	8
5	3	1	9	8	11	5	6	9	6
7	2	9	8	11	13	7	7	4	5
1	7	4	3	5	3	12	3	2	9

<u>2. ANSWERS</u>

Q71	Q72	Q73	Q74	Q75	Q76	Q77	Q78	Q79	Q80
10	5	4	10	6	14	8	12	4	6
1	13	3	2	4	11	9	6	8	11
15	6	6	4	7	10	1	7	5	10
4	8	8	6	3	9	5	11	13	4
2	9	13	11	14	8	14	2	9	7
6	12	7	15	12	2	7	15	11	12
14	14	15	14	11	6	10	10	3	15
9	2	10	7	9	7	13	9	10	5
7	4	5	13	13	3	11	4	14	14
5	1	11	8	1	13	12	5	6	1
8	11	1	9	15	12	4	1	7	2
12	3	2	12	2	15	6	3	2	3
3	10	9	1	8	4	15	8	15	8
11	7	14	5	10	1	2	13	1	9
13	15	12	3	5	5	3	14	12	13

<u>2. ANSWERS</u>

Q81	Q82	Q83	Q84	Q85	Q86	Q87	Q88	Q89	Q90
2	12	6	5	12	13	6	12	3	7
1	10	3	2	11	10	2	10	1	9
10	6	4	6	14	7	4	6	6	4
5	5	10	4	2	2	11	14	12	12
15	13	2	7	1	12	3	7	2	11
4	1	14	14	5	8	5	3	5	1
9	11	5	10	4	6	10	11	8	3
6	14	7	1	13	1	8	5	13	10
14	8	1	9	9	9	13	1	10	2
12	7	8	13	7	5	7	9	9	15
3	15	11	11	8	4	9	4	14	6
8	9	13	15	15	3	15	13	4	13
7	4	9	3	10	11	12	8	11	8
13	2	15	12	3	14	14	2	15	5
1	3	12	8	6	15	1	15	7	14

<u>2. ANSWERS</u>

Q91	Q92	Q93	Q94	Q95	Q96	Q97	Q98	Q99	Q100
8	3	1	5	1	8	5	14	10	5
1	2	12	10	9	11	15	10	2	4
12	6	2	13	8	10	2	11	14	15
5	15	7	8	15	9	10	3	3	14
11	5	8	4	7	14	12	7	8	3
14	13	5	2	5	4	6	13	15	6
7	14	15	11	14	12	8	5	7	8
4	10	6	15	10	7	9	15	11	11
6	9	10	14	3	15	14	4	6	7
13	12	13	3	11	5	7	9	5	10
3	1	3	7	13	6	11	2	13	12
9	8	14	1	12	2	1	8	4	9
2	11	9	9	6	3	13	12	12	2
10	7	11	6	4	1	3	6	9	1
15	4	4	12	2	13	4	1	1	13

3. APPENDIX

WordNet 3.0 license

* 9 7 9 8 5 1 3 7 2 2 4 0 3 *